Knowing Stones: Poems of Exotic Places
[An Anthology]

Compiled and Edited by Maureen Tolman Flannery

John Gordon Burke Publisher, Inc.

Poems in Place Series

Library of Congress Cataloging-in-Publication Data

Knowing stones : poems of exotic places : an anthology / compiled and edited by Maureen Tolman Flannery.

   p. cm. — (Poems in place)

   Includes index.

   ISBN 0–934272–62–X (paper : alk. paper). — ISBN 0–934272–61–1 (cloth : alk. paper)

   1. Antiquities—Poetry. 2. American poetry–20th century. 3. Voyages and travels–Poetry. 4. Poetry of places. 5. Travel–Poetry. I. Flannery, Maureen Tolman, 1947- II. Series.

PS595.A58 K58 2000

811'5080355-dc21   00–040367

Copyright©2000 by John Gordon Burke Publisher, Inc.
All Rights Reserved
Printed and Bound in the United States of America

All poems in this anthology are copyright by the author of the poem or their respective copyright assignees, and are reprinted here with the copyright holder's permission. All poems are the intellectual property of the authors or the respective copyright assignees.

Introduction

I set out to compile a slender volume of poems about archaeological sites such as cromlecks, pyramids, temples, and other ceremonial centers. It seemed a reachable destination, though not without the hazards and surprises of any journey to a remote place. Now, a year later and the expedition completed, I reflect upon how the evolution of this book followed the same road as the special brand of travel it came to represent. In being open to the way the road beckons, the editor, like the traveler, can take detours. Why not arrange a loose schedule to wait for the shadow of equinox sun to undulate like a serpent down pyramid steps, take that side trip with an interesting companion you met at the ruins, or investigate a culture unknown to you before you left home?

Often the most memorable experiences are those not on any itinerary. We have all heard stories of the unanticipated events that defined a trip. Perhaps the mosque your friend had hoped to see was boarded up, the magnificent curve of its dome scored by home-made scaffolding. Yet the holy man waiting outside escorted the stranger to places not noted on a tourist map. So it has been with this anthology. Immersed in the wealth of material submitted, I found certain paths and sites asserting themselves as obvious, essential aspects of the book. The following eight chapters represent these unexpected treasures of the road.

The achievements of ancient peoples have left a compelling record in stone. Among ruins, we view the remains of this former greatness on its way to becoming sand. Its mystery, like a dolmen, balances between timelessness and transience. The massive stones are durable reminders that past civilizations had knowledge and skills we have sacrificed on our path toward the deification of science. In these places that awaken our instinctual reverence, we find some residue of a former intimacy with gods and goddesses that made it possible for our ancestors to create a masonry of worship. Contemplating such sites, we seek an analysis beyond the facts that guidebooks provide. We are fortunate, in this travelogue, to see exotic places keenly observed and transformed through the poetic psyche, which can reorder what seems to be coming apart.

Reading about the world as these poets experienced it, I realized why the poet's genre and the subject of travel seemed a perfect fit. What writer is better suited to examine the journey than the poet who, like the pilgrim, carries wonder to a place and takes home a spark of enlightenment. Everything a poet encounters seems foreign and therefore worthy of close attention, yet reassuringly related, at times in some bizarre fashion, to what is familiar.

In contrast to the sameness of the mundane, ancient wonders draw the seeker away from home and from the understood ways of the time and place that are close at hand. Is it not the human experience to be always in transit between poles of the familiar and the far away, the secure and the exhilaratingly dangerous? The adventurer wants to scale the highest mountain, take part in the most extraordinary ritual, or sail through the most legendary triangle of mystery in the seven seas.

It is no wonder that, having arrived at the exotic, we try to find our bearings in the known. Disoriented, we rely on comparison to steady us from vertigo or provide safe footing at the precipice. What the poet adds to the vagabond's experience is the imaginative link between apparent opposites—metaphor. A poet can take the exotic and present it to us with its duly noted relation to the comfort and predictability of home.

I went on great adventures to wondrous and astonishing places through the words of these poet–travelers. I trust you will too.

Maureen Tolman Flannery

TABLE OF CONTENTS

Chapter One: DRAPE PLACE ON YOUR SHOULDERS AND GO

Cape, Marjorie Maddox	13
In Transit, Elisavietta Ritchie	14
Red is the Color of the Year, Cassie Premo Steele	15
Road to Santipur, Maureen Micus Crisick	16
Stray, Andrew Epstein	18
Dreams of Vagabonds, Maria Quinn	19
Recalling San Ignacio, Bruce Berger	20
Stone with Hole, Christine Swanberg	22
A Woman Can Live by Bread Alone, Vivian Shipley	23
The Coming of Agriculture, Stephen Gibson	25
The Boy Who Dreamed of Building Pompeii, June Owens	26
To Ride the White Camel, Elisavietta Ritchie	28
Not to Be in Basra, Layle Silbert	29
I Don't Know the Local, Don Schofield	30
Without Sun, Without Language, Maureen Micus Crisick	32
Rainy Season, Jonathan Harrington	33

Chapter Two: WHAT THE RUINS REMEMBER

Transformations of Stone, David Lloyd	37
The Stone Circle, Floyd Skloot	38
Sand, Do Gentry	39
Creation at Stonehenge, Diane Engle	40
Salisbury Plain, M. P. A. Sheaffer	41
Megaliths, Deanne Bayer	43
Monument: Avebury Stone Circle, Netta Gillespie	44
Dolmen on the Kilkenny Road, Claire Keyes	45
dysert o–dea, John Knoepfle	46
On Jekyll Island, Enid Shomer	48
Deserted Mansion, Rural South, Netta Gillespie	50
Canyon de Muerte, Sharon Scholl	51
A Short Way, Las Ruinas de Chichén Itzá, Katie Kingston	52
Journey to the Maya, Gladys Swan	53
Pacal's Tomb, Margaret Blaker	55

Monument: Coba, Netta Gillespie	56
Notes from the Inca Trail, Michael Gill	57
Stones of the Sacred Valley of the Incas, Maria Quinn	59
Quipu Song, Near the Top, Ruth Moon Kempher	61
The Theatre of Epidaurus, Joseph Powell	63
Among Ruins, Joseph A. Soldati	64
Pythagoras Academy, Rina Ferrarelli	66
Aninoüs and the Charioteer, Rina Ferrarelli	67
Mary's House Near Ephesus, Anthony Russell White	68
At the Ruins of San Simeon in September, Sandy Feinstein	69
Ain Dara, Sandy Feinstein	70
Footprints at the Temple at Ain Dara, Syria, Ann Struthers	71
A Street in Cairo, Sandra Goldsmith	72
Ancient Egypt Is Behind You, Amy Stewart	73
An Egyptian Evening, Steve Barfield	74
At the Great Zimbabwe Ruins, Christopher Conlon	76
Walking the Wall, Phillis Gershator	78
The Great Wall, William Wei-Yi Marr	80
A Gift of Two Stones, For Mr. Liang, John Calvin Rezmerski	81
The Western Wall, Dale Sprowl	82
From the Wailing Wall, Enid Shomer	84
Reading the Stones, Elisavietta Ritchie	85

Chapter Three: *LOVE AMONG THE RUINS*

Stone Lemons, W. K. Buckley	89
First Crossing, Jody Bolz	91
Eileen Munda, Darrell g.h. Schramm	94
Rising and Falling, Leza Lowitz	95
First Anniversary Pantoum, Richard Beban	98
The Lost Civilization, Michael Waters	100
In India the Stone Temple Gods, Richard Beban	101
Flesh and Spirit, Diane Lutovich	102
Passion Conch, Michael Waters	103
Carry Home What You Can, Andrew Epstein	105
At Night Your Mouth, Kelly Cherry	106
The Kiss, Elliot Richman	108
Shadows of Moremi, Susan Terris	110
The Day We Saw the Elephant, Jacqueline Kudler	111

At Arthur's Stone, William Greenway	112
In the Viennese Style, Enid Shomer	114
Taormina, Sicily, Kathleen Iddings	115
The Train Ride to Moscow, Dale Sprowl	116
The Conjure Woman, Carolyne Wright	117
Translating Lourdes, Douglas W. Lawder	119
Presage at Machu Picchu, Rose Rosberg	120
Machu Picchu, Rainy Season, Maria Quinn	121
Will You Take Me into Death with You, Elliot Richman	122
Plans for a House in Latvia, Kelly Cherry	124
In Kraljevo, Elisavietta Ritchie	125
Wayang, Jody Bolz	126

Chapter Four: THE LAND KEEPS UNHOLY SECRETS

Sheep, Anna Citrino	131
Prosthesis Factory in Phnom Penh, Tom McCarthy	133
The Hotel Cambodiana, Willa Schneberg	135
Soweto, Christopher Conlon	136
At the Senbitsuka, Leza Lowitz	138
Shadow Poem, Deborah Byrne	139
The Taro Fields, Claire T. Feild	140
Carib's Leap, Andrew Epstein	141
Scapegoats, Carol Kanter	143
Stealing Blackberries at Port Arthur, Elisavietta Ritchie	144
Of Barracks and Bee Stings, Sandra Olson	146
Report from an Unnamed City, Kelly Cherry	147
Livadiya Palace, Site of the Yalta Conference, Kelly Cherry	148
Russian Parliament 8/20/91, Walter Bargen	149
Prague's Revenge, Michele Battiste	150
Sarajevo, Elisavietta Ritchie	151
Lorca at the Wall, Steve Barfield	153
Poland, 1990, Alan Elyshevitz	154
Berlin Wall, Leza Lowitz	155
Dos Marias, Cassie Premo Steele	156
Underworld Palace Scene with Beheading, Margaret Blaker	157
Between Cartegena and Baranquilla, Darrell g.h. Schramm	158
Smile, Jonathan Harrington	159

The Room, Carolyne Wright   160
Keeping Watch: on Route to Brazil, M. Eliza Hamilton Abegunde   163

Chapter Five: OH, THE PEOPLE YOU'LL MEET

On the Chao Phraya, Bangkok, Thea Sullivan   167
"Night in the Tropics" (1858-59?), Michael Waters   168
Our Lady of the Pigeons, Richard Beban   169
Woman Knitting Over Florence, Bill Yake   170
Maxwell Street, Margaret Mantle   171
Phnom Penh Street, Tom McCarthy   173
Andean Snapshot, Hallie Moore   175
On a Plane from Cuzco, Maria Quinn   176
Riding the Coffin, Tyler Enfield   178
The Miracle Room, Carolyne Wright   179
The Ballroom, Christopher Conlon   181
Egyptian Time, David Radavich   182
Echoes of a Native Land, John Dickson   183
Island Dance, Don Schofield   184
Mosaic, Ashley Mace Havird   185
The Rug Dealer, Joy E. Stocke   187
Printmaking: Wiping an Inked Plate, Pearl Karrer   189
The Spanish Boys at the Hotel Manx, Deborah Byrne   190
Alchemist Michael Sendivogius Conducts a Tour of Prague,
  John Gilgun   192
From Botswana to Zanzibar, Walter Bargen   194
Mac Donnchadha, Tour Guide, John Gilgun   196
Eulogia, Fichard Fammerée   198
Them, Elisavietta Ritchie   200

Chapter Six: WATER FLOWS OVER OUR KNOWING

Bermuda Triangle, Sharon Scholl   203
Ninety-Eight Point Six, Dale Sprowl   205
Even in the Worst of Light, Lynda Calabrese   206
Phosphorescent Bay: Vieques, Marilyn Zuckerman   207
Night Vision, Daniel Green   208
Lapakahi, Hawaii, Alan Elyshevitz   209
A Tourist Counts on Stone to Save Her, Karen Douglass   210
Mont-Saint-Michel, Margaret Mantle   211

Dawn at Sligo Bay, Floyd Skloot	213
Cabo San Lucas Bay, Lorraine Tolliver	214
La Paz, Maureen Micus Crisick	216
The River, Ann Sylvester	217
Through Breezes of Chanta Palms, Linda Casebeer	218
The Killing Jar, Linda Casebeer	219
Tree Tops, Linda Casebeer	220
The Arctic Cycle, Deanne Bayer	221

Chapter Seven: WE TAKE THE DEAD ALONG OR MEET THEM THERE

On Seeing the Dead Walk, Susan Terris	225
The Seamstress, Leza Lowitz	226
Travelogue at Glacier Bay, Carol Kanter	227
notes from a journey, John Knoepfle	229
The Oracle of Delphi, Gary Mex Glazner	230
Evora (A Song), Richard Fammerée	232
To the Field of Reeds, Enid Shomer	234
Requiem, Tom Roby	236
Amaryllis, Deborah Byrne	237
What the Heart Weighs (In the Catacombs, Paris 1997), Richard Beban	238
Michaelskirche, Vienna, Bill Yake	240
Divisions, Lynore G. Banchoff	241
The Body Can Ascend No Higher, Paulette Roeske	242
Visiting the Dead, Laurence Snydal	243
The Barber Surgeon's Death Bertha Rogers	244
Self–Burial, William Greenway	245
Burying Babies in Indonesia, Kate Gray	247
The Well of Sacrifice, James Doyle	248
The Civilized Sacrifice, Walter Bargen	250
The Mummy of Aconcagua, Shelly Berc	251

Chapter Eight: ALTAR STONES WILL ALTER YOU

Eulene Between Acts, Carolyne Wright	255
The Road to Muktinath, Sandra Olson	257
The Faces at Braga, David Whyte	259
Prambanan, Java, Jody Bolz	261
The Enlightened One, Glenna Holloway	262

In Kamakura (Japan), Jeffrey Loo	263
Horus' Eye, Carol Nolde	264
Olduvai, Sharon Scholl	266
Floating Over Kala–Llit–Nunaati, Anthony Russell White	267
Ingenue in Bali, Rose Rosberg	268
Reflections at Newgrange, Kathy Kennedy Tapp	269
Daughters, Kathleen Cain	270
Alseep in Ireland, Richard Fammerée	271
All That You Need, She Says, Kathleen Cain	273
Nottingham, Madeleine Beckman	275
Granada, Deanne Bayer	276
Pressure Points, Tom Roby	278
Easter in Aegina, Joseph Powell	280
Aztecs, B. A. St. Andrews	282
Ruins, Jonathan Harrington	284
Mayan Pyramid, Yucatan Peninsula, John Gilgun	285
For My Best Friend, Who Has Seen Miracles, Richard Beban	286
Treasures, Jonathan Harrington	288

Contributors 289

Acknowledgments 305

Index 310

Drape Place on Your Shoulders and Go

Each of us has felt an impulse that wells up and whispers that it's time to travel again. A longing for the exotic begins to stir when the familiar feels like a yoke that must be shaken off. Soon this vague calling crescendos to a dictate that we go. And, in the going, distinctions between body and landscape blur. Those who listen to the voice and set out for the unknown soon become cloaked in the bright world and will go home differently dressed.

Unusual places exist, not only on the map, but in the imaginations of individuals who dream of sun-bleached cities, unique beasts of mythical beauty, or exquisite foods to nourish the hungry. Some towns are so peaceful they tug at the sleeve, enticing the rover to forget about leaving. But one who is on the move must keep up with the life that lies ahead.

Marjorie Maddox

CAPE

What doesn't fit is
loose enough to move
in. Drape place on your shoulders and go.
Inflated: a map with beret,
your fabric–skin thick
enough. To twirl,
spin wind where the sleeves aren't.
Lift yourself. It's latitude you like.
Who says there are four winds
only? Fast–pitch caution. Breeze or
tornado—one is the other
sometime. You know where
the sun is. Even melted,
you're a flat felt globe, tilting.

Author's Note: My work is informed by questions of how we cross over or are confined by boundaries of place and body.

Elisavietta Ritchie

IN TRANSIT

Coming from somewhere else
at any age, even *in utero,*
you're never sure

your feet touch the soil.
Your whole life you hover—
hawk, helicopter

or fat dirigible, fearful
someone might poke a hole,
light a match—

You hang in there, up there,
wondering will they finally
grant permission to land

or forever challenge your passport,
check your fingerprints,
discount your money, question

could you survive as a stranger?
Best stay suspended,
forget the keys to the town.

Here, the air is dangerous, cold,
wind currents tricky, but
God, what a view.

Author's Note: This poem was the first poem to come while I was traveling all over Australia with my husband Clyde Farnsworth, who was covering the country for the *New York Times*. My father, a Russian émigré, was in the U.S. Army during World War II. When I was a child we moved an average of once a year. As an adult I have lived in Cyprus, Lebanon, and Malaysia, as well as the U.S. and Canada, and much of my life, literally and figuratively, has been spent en route to somewhere else.

Cassie Premo Steele

RED IS THE COLOR OF THE YEAR

Red is the color of the year
when, with great sadness,
you will leave your bags in doorways
of your life, and hail a trail,
and not look back at what you leave behind,

and laugh, and let the path come to take you
You will go to the land *de flor y canto*.
Do not give up if at first
you do not find them.
Keep walking. Keep crying. Keep believing

in your voice. It will lead you
to the corner of a thousand red carnations.
Buy a dozen. Buy red *chiles*. Smell them both.
They are the smell of your new life.

Author's Note: The land *"de flor y canto"* is the land of flower and song, Mexico, where this poem was written.

Maureen Micus Crisick

ROAD TO SANTIPUR

You could leave the kitchen where you've knelt
in homage to burnt toast. Close the dusty drapes.
Light is mute, wrote Dante.
Leave the washroom where your father's
voice lives in each stain.

Fill your suitcase with palette knives,
fresh tubes of paint to practice
who you never were. Fuchsias blooming
in the atrium are blinded by their own beauty.
Ants crawling on the dead bee
have a singleness of purpose.

While there's still time, before your hands
wrinkle to fig, walk past the office humdrum,
its Xerox machines duplicating, duplicating,
past boulevards of chrome cars imitating
riches. Where water begins, cross
the ropebridge and go far into the world
with its many terraces. Notice reeds poking
like hair through green skin of scum.
By tomorrow, you could wake near a slow fire,
put on hemp sandals, pour saffron tea and watch
its arc fill with light. Already the sun
is in the curve of your spoon.

If you open your notebook, a hawk will
rise up, circling in the ageless heat,
stunned by your resolve. But first, the eye
must go inward. *Nature's inside,* said Cezanne.
Early light is untroubled, permits itself
anything: wild luminosity of a woman bathing
in the sea, cranes of her kimono left
to preen on the shore.

Knowing Stones

Near the banyan tree, its long legs
rooted in swamp, turn the sunning stone over
for its dark amnesia. You, on the edge
of your white dream: the bare bone of paper
still desires you. What matters is the immensity

of sky and that one bird cries in affirmation.

Author's Note: Abandon your day-to-day and journey into the exotic world of your own creativity. Santipur is one of the strange and lovely places along that road.

Andrew Epstein

STRAY

In mid–August it rains and it is time to go.
I've known it all my life: how the sad paths
would curl out from our blue door, how the bushes
where I tumbled as a boy would recede,
one endless background growing all the time.

In constant rain I feel the weight

we load on our poised parents, their leafy suburban homes
filled with empty rooms aching like
the places in the gum where teeth once were.

In Italy, we talked our way through the ruins,
summoning a future amid all that crumbled past.

The light was rich and rose and olive and the stones
were scattered, silent.
We saw cat after cat, strays,
all muscle and gut and sheer will

stalking about the bare monuments, homeless and angry.
I sat where an emperor's son grabbed his sword and books
and ran from home.
I kicked stones washed by a river of Roman mothers' tears.

I'm leaving now to forget what I never understood,
the mystery of family, to spread myself
like a cat spreads its scent
on all the sharp edges of the world,

my life dashing before me like a mouse. Don't look back.
Ignore the ruins. Pounce.

Author's Note: The Forum in Rome, Italy.

Maria Quinn

DREAMS OF VAGABONDS

keep falling on the wrong pillow.
Arriving in time–frames of life in warm climates,
they lurch, disoriented, into some other restless psyche
on a hard bench in a train station far from anywhere,
insinuate themselves into a stranger's arrangements
in the previous pensión,
or hovel, before dawn, above an empty cot
in some mountain town hostel.
Often out of synch, the dreams of vagabonds
might reach them in *la madrugada*
in a language they are trying to forget.

Author's Note: *La madrugada* refers to the early, pre–dawn hours of the morning.

Bruce Berger

RECALLING SAN IGNACIO

Is it the desert burning beyond this breeze
That makes the date palms sing
In the shallow canyon? Great laurel trees
Plunge the plaza in cool
And with a dull cracked ring
The mission bell invites a more ancient shade,
Although there's no padre now.
Before your steps have pulled you a hundred feet
The peace sinks into your veins and, drawn
From the clays of one quiet street
To the next, you stumble over your rule
Against staying; obscurely you vow
To return and, like any traveler, push on.

The water springs for some reason of its own
Out of the desert clay
And runs a few miles through stream, lagoon
And palm–lined reservoir,
Its arteries nourishing on the way
Gardens and orchards tangled in high ferment
Over settlements bleached with lime,
Then vanishes into the sunbaked earth like the night
Swallowing some half–imagined flame;
Just so creation might
Have sprung from the infinite nowhere,
To burst itself into brilliant
Shades along a meander of time
And dissolve again near a place from which it came.

Knowing Stones

Beauty seldom takes root. Yet someday
A man stepping off to explore
The unknown's edge and on his way
Watching his planet fall
Through stellar dark until it's no more
Than remembered muscat on the vine of space,
And sick with the lust to see
Around the next bend and stamp it with his name,
May long for a corner where he spent
A moment's peace with the same
Longing a traveler might recall
San Ignacio, a place
Buried inside himself where he
Might drink from a satisfied heart, and be content.

Author's Note: The village of San Ignacio, in Mexico's Baja California Sur, began as the Cochimi oasis of Kadakaamán, "place of the reeds," and was developed into a mission settlement by Jesuits and Dominicans. The Indians died of contracted diseases, and current inhabitants have descended from Spanish soldiers and mestizos brought there by missionaries.

Christine Swanberg

STONE WITH HOLE

    you will find me
   holding up the pillars
of Chichén Itzá or Alexandria
i am the parrot's eye of Easter Island
    17 Indians polished me
    ground out this hole
which you peer through now
  the curve in my side
  is like the curve in yours
    your dry hip bone
  bleached   gleaming
   in another world

Author's Note: In 1975, Mexico, Guatemala, and Belize were not as accessible as they are now. Reaching the many archaeological wonders was an arduous task which involved rickety buses, wooden boats and half-cocked DC-3's in the political unrest of Guatemala and Belize.

Vivian Shipley

A WOMAN CAN LIVE BY BREAD ALONE

> "I get it all from earth my daily bread."
> –Tony Harrison

Imagine, me in England. The White Crusty,
the Cut and the Uncut. The Small Tin,
the Large Tin, the Bloomer. A cottage loaf,
round, white and bouncy like feather pillows,

down filled mattresses and if the topknot
is missing, I'll be teething a farmer's loaf
dusted with flour. If I finger square corners,
four by eight inches, brown, light, smooth,

not grainy, I will know for sure it's Hovis.
Ciabatta and brioche found their way
across the English Channel. So can I.
For a change of pace, picture me in India.

Let's say Bombay for the caption. I will stuff
chapati, phulka so hot it burns my tongue,
tandoori nan and the even sweeter Frontier
version, Peshawari nan, in my mouth all at once.

Overloaded? Not until I eat reshmi roti,
the shirmal, the paratha will I have the need
to compensate for the sin of over indulgence.
Simplify, me in Karachi, Pakistan. No servant.

Backdropped by dawn, I wait in line for a loaf
outside the Monastery of the Angels' stone wall.
Baked by the nuns to honor God, the bread is
rationed as if there were a war. No bulk buying.

Stuffed with money, my pockets will be emptied
for a few bites of crust. A hatch opens. My head
must be bowed, my eyes averted while I file
past, right hand extended as if I were a sinner

sticking out her tongue for communion's grace.
A wooden tray slides out with my allotted bread,
white, soft, light like the wings of an angel surely
will be, floating me to what heaven can be had.

Author's Note: My major problem in caring for my father who has cancer is to get him to eat. He loves bread and wants it in some form with every meal. I bake him biscuits and cornbread for variety. While feeding him, I thought of how many types of bread there are and how it is a central food in all cultures. The Monastery of the Angels reference suggested the religious significance of bread.

Stephen Gibson

THE COMING OF AGRICULTURE

for Clorinda

Walled cities, acres deep, clay
shaped and bricked, baked, laced with straw,
slapped and molded, the same as bread dough
kneaded with your fingers making pizza—
which must sit, covered with a moist cloth,
dead in its cerements for an hour,
and then rise: the miracle you expect
happens, because the sequence of actions
to be followed is memory, ritual, the initiation
into mysteries only learned by example
(unlike receipts, which are written down;
hence, the preponderance of clay tablets
found at Sumer noting exchange:
30 cattle, 40 sheep, 3 hectares of land
surveyed for tax purposes). Witness
my surprise when we came to Pompeii
eight years ago (tourist that I am,
fumbling for the right phrase,
talking to strangers): the shapes of the loaves
found in the ovens when the city died
are recognized as yours—even
to the four air-vents cut at the top.
They were left there in haste when Vesuvius
blew, the oven doors unopened for centuries,
until some other hand cut shafts
into the hillside tumuli, which resemble
the loaves turned to charcoal in the ovens—
perfectly round at the base, flattened at the top.
"The largest single step in the ascent of man
is the change from nomad to village agriculture"
—Jacob Bronowski. Though flatworms
plowed acres through their anuses,
obliterating the city and the memory of the city,
still, the first agricultural settlement
is known: a pregnant woman, kneading bread dough.

Author's Note: When my wife and I visited the ruins of Pompeii, I was struck by the charred loaves of bread, some still on the baker's peel. My wife Clorinda could probably trace her ancestry back to that city, or one nearby. How often I had watched her kneading dough, forming loaves of the same shape. The similarity spoke to me of continuity, endings and also beginnings, for after that trip to Italy we started a family.

June Owens

THE BOY WHO DREAMED OF BUILDING POMPEII

I shall build a city of houses
So white the sun will be blinded
And the moon will move
More slowly through night,
Perfecting itself in my city's perfection.
And when the foothilled land is levelled,
I shall insist, Hortensia, that small trees
Be left standing—olive and wild fig,
Cypresses and Lombardy poplars.
Each house will have running water.
Yes. And a rainpool, a little fountain.
And ... and ... music in the marble,
Coming from nowhere but the wind,
While women play chance–games,
Tossing human knucklebones.
At every door, urns of geraniums.
Small gardens of melissa and basil,
Hyssop and oregano. At every window,
Loops of strung garlic swaying.
Corinthian columns, inside, not out,
Will divide space into shadows.
There will be terrazzo floors, niches
For images of loved ones, entire rooms
Done in mosaic, with sweet–scented oil lamps,
And walls painted with pictures of false
Windows whose vineyards and vistas—
Eternal, marvelous–leap gently out
Of the outer world into atriums
Of silent coolness; and friezes, Octavius,
So beautiful ... so beautiful, mysterious,
Outrageous and wicked they will
Spellbind centuries of men.

Knowing Stones

From afar, my city will be seen as though
It were water on which the sun shines,
Or like the snows of northern Italy when ice
Lies love–making and crystalized upon it.
Oh, I shall build a city so bright
And wondrous, my disbelievers,
That Vesuvius will die in mid–eruption
For love of her.

Author's Note: Ancient Pompeii was destroyed by an eruption of Mt. Vesuvius in A.D. 79. Years ago an arts professor/friend took a sabbatical at Pompeii and brought to me a small stone from one of its streets. In writing the poem, I simply let that little stone speak to me.

Elisavietta Ritchie
TO RIDE THE WHITE CAMEL

Wait in silence while all
the beige, brown and gray
camels lumber away from the well.

Wait in silence
on beige, brown, gray sand
until the white camel approaches.

She also waits.
Offer fresh dates
from the palm overhead.

If she accepts, weave jasmine
flowers into her bridle.
Lead her toward the rushing

channel of water
along the clay aqueduct.
Fill your amphora upstream.

When the white camel kneels,
grasp the pommel of olive wood,
spring up and over, onto the saddle.

She hoists herself up
like an earthquake.
Apologize for the burden.

When she stops in the pomegranate grove
reach for the rosiest fruit.
Split the skin with your nails

When you reach the cactus fence,
if the white camel wishes,
proceed into the desert.

Do not be certain
either of you
will return.

Continue across the Sahara
eating the pomegranate
seed by infinite seed.

Author's Note: I did. In Tunisia. I had ridden camels on Cyprus and in Jordan, but none was as delicate and beautiful as this Tunisian lady.

Layle Silbert

NOT TO BE IN BASRA

not their affair   we decide
not to answer   what is your religion
on the visa form
coming into Basra
not a scheduled stop
on the way to Cairo
not allowed to board again
to be taken in
not for not answering
but for what they think
belongs in that empty space
not for a life of crime
not for acts of terror   for being
not born into the right religion

Abe leaves to argue our case
I wait in the airport lounge
not wanted and alone
not allowed to go outside
from the open door I see
Basra shimmering in ancient sunlight
not ever to know
the three women walking in black chodors
not to see Iraq
not the hanging gardens of Babylon
not to know if we'd ever go
I buy a wooden box of hand-packed dates
wait for Abe

Author's Note: When our plane made an unscheduled stop in Basra, Iraq my husband and I were singled out for attention because of difficulties then between Israel and Iraq, even though we were Americans, not Israelis.

Don Schofield

I DON'T KNOW THE LOCAL

word for that ridge,
   these steppes,
      those tall

thin evergreens here
   and there across this valley,
      the flock of sparrows racing

as if to slam into
   a wall, veering
      at the last instant

up into the dusk sky;
   no name
      for the back-lit figs, the tufts

of dangling grass, this path I walk
   to town, so I veer
      inward

to flint emotions
   which also can't be named,
      syntax felt

as one lone tree
   turning its leaves against
      impending rain;

no story
   to distinguish me
      from the world I pass through:

white ridge of my mother's arms?
   deep ditch of my father's
      last look? stiff

Knowing Stones

    tufts of a self
        I've lost? Am I
            this man passing on a donkey,

    two cows with sloped backs
        behind him, one white
            as his scarf, the other

    dirty brown like his pants? He waves.
        I grin and point to the sky,
            say the one word I know

    too fast. I want to cover this valley
        with words he understands,
            but I can't even gesture clearly.

    He points a thick finger
        down to the ground as his donkey
            brays its long

    abrasive lament,
        then they turn to a field
            of scrub, the cows

    following without being led,
        sparrows jabbering
            as they dive into some darkening

    tree while I turn again
        to this unnamed path—all of us
            turning and turning

    on local earth.

Author's Note: During my first year in Greece, I lived for several months in a remote village on the island of Lesbos (Mytilene). During that time I was struggling to orient myself emotionally and psychologically in the landscape and culture of a place that I would eventually call home.

Maureen Micus Crisick

WITHOUT SUN, WITHOUT LANGUAGE

The landlord is drunk again. *Vizlat*
his voice brings winter.

Downstairs, a quarrel in Hungarian.
Lunatic rage rises

with odors of fish. I am drowning
in words not my own, a black water.

Ez Zarva! workers hiss to one another
from rooftops ragged with ice.

I stand at the window, unable to interpret
the sudden rain. Clouds disfigure the sky.

I throw away newspapers I cannot read,
their cold forest of vowels.

Tonight in my iron bed I need dreams
in a language I remember as my own.

I need to return to my garden,
its blood–hot tomatoes, hear my daughters'

news of the day, transparent talk, sweet noise,
their picnic of words spread out in clear light.

Author's Note: I spent a dark, post-Communist winter in Siofok, Hungary, living alone, teaching in isolation among a wilderness of strangers.

Jonathan Harrington

RAINY SEASON

Almost thirty years old
and this is my life—
this room in this city
in a country thousands of miles
from my birthplace.
Sparsely furnished as a cell,
piles of books on the floor,
papers, bills, official documents
that define my existence.
Three mounds of coins
each in a separate currency.
Two packages of pills:
dysentery, malaria.
Diseases I once thought happened
only in Tarzan movies
now seem as common as a headache.
My boots stare up at me
like hungry mouths
and my clothes are piled
on the tile floor.
A hammock swings lazily
under the easy wind
of an overhead fan
and a bleeding Jesus
looks down
from the wall.
A desk, an old typewriter
and a sheaf of my poems,
coffee-stained, unread,
and curling from the rainy season.
Outside, I hear the fruit vendors shouting
and the clop-clop of horse hooves
on the brick street.

The sounds, now familiar,
make me wonder
how we ever get where we are?
And how, in God's name,
do we get back home?

Author's Note: I spent a year writing in Merida, Yucatan, surrounded by Maya ruins, colonial achitecture, caves and beaches. "Rainy Season" is a meditation on the unexplained reasons why we end up living where we do.

What the Ruins Remember

Ruins represent the petrified stories of ancient peoples. We walk among them seeking knowledge by proximity, wondering what memories they withhold. Despite the fact that we are drawn to them, as to all things mysterious, they guard their secrets jealously, knowing more than their seemingly mute faces will divulge. Yet poets refer to the language of stone, its poetry, and the eloquence of its silence. In the crenated surface is imbedded centuries of the songs of wind and water.

Standing stones, pyramids, temples, cathedrals and mosques have become fossilized prayers that uplift the spirit. Whoever goes to these sites with questions might be serenaded by their silent voices. Filled with wonder, a visitor becomes a convert to the religion of rock, and may leave with even more questions.

David Lloyd

TRANSFORMATIONS OF STONE

Giants who walk the earth
become stones in graves

of tangled root
and soil, become loose boulders

we lift for our
design, or scree,

or shards on the hill slope
of the axe–factory,

or axe–head,
or broken axe–head buried

in a stranger's skull, or the capstone
of that one's rich grave,

or his whetstone, his amulet,
his scythe, his private wealth,

or a public cromlech for the sun
to site men excavating

open air temples,
or become the air itself,

moving in secret ways
over hills and stones.

Author's Note: This is the title poem of a sequence that takes as its subject the Neolithic and Bronze Age standing stones, burial chambers, and stone circles of Wales. The ancient monuments are often situated with commanding views of valleys, mountains, and coasts. The remains of this Neolithic axe factory are located on a mountain slope near Penmaenmawr, north Wales.

Floyd Skloot

THE STONE CIRCLE

Clouds mass behind Slievemore
and cast the mountain's shifting
shadow across the valley floor.
We watch sunlit heather change
from pink to indigo as though
drained and veins of peat vanish
where turf was cut. Now gorse
grows purple, bruised by sudden
shifts in weather. As light falls
apart before our eyes, color drifts
away on winds that siphon
the last blue off Lough Keel
and bury Inishgalloon in fine mist.
We sit in silence on stone
slabs placed here in the late
Bronze Age. Three mountain sheep
with scarlet dye in their fleece
move upslope toward crumbling
cottages and suddenly everything
is bathed in a cataract of gold.

Author's Note: On Achill Island, off the west coast of Ireland, where my wife and I spent a summer, there was a deserted village half a mile from our cottage. This cluster of collapsed stone buildings on the slopes of Slievemore had been used by families who spent the summers letting their cattle graze the mountainside. In and amongst the abandoned buildings lay a stone circle dating from the Bronze Age.

Do Gentry

SAND

The smooth rock that shifts unexpectedly
beneath your feet, the smooth one
you carry in your pocket.
The rock with the white stripe
like a ribbon tied around a velvet box.

The single loosened pebble
that tumbles over and over
in a cloud of pink dust,
down the steep granite face of the cliff,
becoming the sand everything is becoming.

The rock with leaves stenciled
on its back like folded wings.

The rock that is quarried and cut
and hauled a long way,
then pushed up into place
using levers and complex mathematics.

Or simply lifted upright in the darkness,
who knows how:
willed perhaps,
or sung into place.

Author's Note: "Sand" is from a series called "The Lewis Poems." The island of Lewis is part of the Outer Hebrides of Scotland. This rocky landscape is the oldest exposed stone on earth. The island has numerous prehistoric megaliths, including the Calanais standing stones.

Diane Engle

CREATION AT STONEHENGE

Brace for disappointment, you who travel far toward
no ancient jewels for crowns, no castles,
buried cities,

secret tombs. What answers lie beneath these stones,
scribblings of history in its infancy,
are haunted by ghosts

of prehistoric pain. Perhaps they signal embryos
among the stars or seed
new worlds,

start fresh creations spinning for the wise among
old, restless gods to play with.
Drunk with surprise,

the Adam and Eve of countless Edens can re–abandon
Paradise. Reaching from dust
to meteor, the stones

of centuries lean into heaven, praising those who stand
in stubborn counterpoint to chance beneath
their shadow. If chance

should boast, "I'm master of the stones, a joke the past
plays on the present," let those who come
here humbly bring

their strength to art, set stones among the centuries,
whisper and cry in winter wind,
and sometimes sing.

Author's Note: I am fortunate to have visited Stonehenge before the ropes sealed it off from the crowds. Able to touch and walk among the stones, I was deeply impressed by these massive testaments to the past, and contrived in my own mind an alternative to the usual explanation that such arrangements of stone were erected as astronomical devices, or burial sites.

M. P. A. Sheaffer

Salisbury Plain

Did they emerge from the ferns
Of Wales? From hillsides thick
With pines as ancient as the stones?
From clearings near a stream
That sometimes ran with red?
Who called those stones
To Wiltshire,
Far from the oak and mistletoe
Of Celtic haunts
To nearby Woodhenge?
Who roped the rocks—
A priest? a subaltern?
And did they chant a charm
To keep the stones content
As they were uprooted one by one
From their Gallic glades
And floated toward
An alien plain
To ring around in
A stony cosmic dance
With the solstice secret
In its heel?
And did the priestess swag
Each Sarcen stone with oak
And mistletoe
When the sun broke first
Upon the needle point and splintered light,
Marking off each one
Like minute strokes on a watchface?

And when the last white–robed Druid left,
Did he kneel for one last time
In that grey twilight
Within the circle of the rocks
To hear them sing of home?

Author's Note: One night, driving back to London from Somerset, I saw the sun's last rays create a sheen across Salisbury Plain. Etched in backlight, Stonehenge's great stone circle crowned the crest of the horizon. I was thankful at that point that man had not yet marred this stretch of beauty, because raging around newsprint was the controversy about a new highway that would threaten the environment, possibly even the foundation, of this magnificent site/sight.

Deanne Bayer

MEGALITHS

Stone
is not liturgy—

we have been here
for so long
whoever we were
steeps in lethe, our souls
invested
in images
of abstractions
and the passing
worship
of light—

we have been here
for so long
whatever ideal
was deity
has abraded
to sands
spilling time

and though
what set us here
has been subsumed
in forgetfulness, the ethos
remains
ingrained
somewhere in the shadow
of the stone.

Author's Note: We visited Stonehenge before it was cordoned off, and I still thrill to the awe and wonder that captured me as I walked among these mysterious stones.

Netta Gillespie

MONUMENT: AVEBURY STONE CIRCLE

Stones advance like gray nuns.
After these years, the rock
Is ripe for carving. Shapes
Have retreated inward.
Something more of our time
Struggles toward light.
They are women, weighed down
By heavy veils. Gouged eyes
Have stared the sculptor's
Hand to stone. Branched
Fingers of bone reach, grief
Sighs in leaves. Nothing
On the horizon but bare universe
Clamping the ground. At night
White ghosts condense, float—
Silence gleams in the moon–
Bleached sky. Speak to us.
You know something we must
Know, too. Just a little more
Carving and we could see you.

Author's Note: Avebury Stone Circle, in Wiltshire, dates back to Neolithic Britain. In moonlight, the stones take on ghostly shapes, and many of them (however they were intended) appear as statues of women, which I prefer to think of as half completed rather than half destroyed.

Claire Keyes

DOLMEN ON THE KILKENNY ROAD

How can we tell the stones
from their sadness   each one weighted
into the earth   and each other
like mourners at a funeral
an arm across a shoulder   a son
trying to comfort   his mother
a mother leaning   into a daughter

What makes them   impervious
to decay   Is it the balance
of heft upon heft   the way
the sun darts clean
as a snake's tongue
between crevices   the light
penetrating to the center
at precisely the time   Earth shifts
its enormous bulk

Around us   there's a shiver
of loneliness   the fields bordering
the dolmen   rimmed by a highway
where trucks run fast   to Kilkenny
and we stop   at the Dolmen Mobil
to check the tires   the attendant
with one molar   missing   from the side
of his smile   everything   about this
rock–bedecked island   missing something
and I find a place   inside myself
room for the long stones   and the past
rising   so hard and   clean
out of the green earth

Author's Note: This particular site is but one of many sprinkled throughout the British Isles and northern Europe. Unlike the splendid array of stones at Stonehenge, this small group speaks of the utter normalcy and pervasiveness of these ritual spaces for the ancient Celts.

John Knoepfle

dysert o–dea

a high cross here and it has
a grouchy abbot on it and he is
bigger than the christ in flowers
stretched out above him

or is this saint tola
would have been bemused
old man who came here
and that was in the seven hundreds
getting rid of himself
rid of the noise of the world
some coptic desire in him
burrowing out of the sands of egypt

this church came later
and recobbled from ruins still later
romanesque perhaps
the south door shouldn't be where it is
and those heads beading the arch
what are they with animals thrown in
for someones good measure or bad judgment

the heads are so many trophies
their jaws look wired shut
the mouths turned down
and who are they you would question
saints or sinners the cross captured
some habit from the grand wars
the old celts with their trophies
smothered in oil in cedar boxes

Knowing Stones

      there is no order here
      new graves jumbled with the old
      like some ancient battlefield
      the obriens and leclares spilled blood on
      well there are burial rights it seems
      here where the great great grandfather
      was denied his worship

      the roof is long gone
      only an ancient sky
      exults above this pile of stone

Author's Note: Here in Ireland Saint Tola founded a monastery in the 8th century. The church dates from the 11th century, with a botched 14th century restoration.

Enid Shomer

ON JEKYLL ISLAND

The marker says "Tabby Ruin"
        and we get out of the car to see
                the unstoppered walls,

a hearth shaped like a mouthful
        of ashes. Overhead, the sky
                pours in like history,

so much light, so little
        form. "Tabby" was the local
                concrete, a porridge

of sand and shells dug from Indian
        mounds. Everywhere the stucco
                has flaked, oyster shucks

claw toward us, the hands
        of slaves who bent to the Sea
                Island cotton

that foamed up in this marsh
        like a hundred–year tide.
                I have been reading about the Grand

Tours of the Europeans: they loved
        to be photographed jauntily
                posed with classical

ruins. A century before the camera,
        they painted the fantasy: afternoon
                picnics in a tame

wood, a small orchestra playing,
        the minuet danced before
                broken Roman columns.

Knowing Stones

    Here the Africans sang of thorn
        plants that would bleed
            the color from their

skin. Most of them never set foot
        in this house that now feels less
            somebody's home

than a temple where weather
        is part of the worship
            and the accidental is taken

for fate. Even in the painting
        where the shot stag is propped
            among acanthus

leaves and the gentlemen ride
        a fallen pediment,
            their stockinged calves

the same incandescent peach
        as the sky, the eye is drawn
            finally

upward, to the only monumental
        they or we are sure of—
            the clouds moving by like worn

signets, though we never touch
        them, though we know them only
            from pages and pages of rain.

Author's Note: What remains of the Horton–Dubingnon Plantation is now a roofless ruin. Jekyll Island is one of the sea islands off the coast of Georgia, home of sea island cotton, which was highly prized in the ante–bellum period.

Netta Gillespie

DESERTED MANSION, RURAL SOUTH

When houses stand empty so long
They get hopelessly gray. Sap
Drains from their timbers, and
The oil of life. Fallen statues
Of strange gods with frost–
Cracked faces litter the lawns.
Slowly, slowly, time eats the doors,
Love stands in the window
Holding tattered curtains over
Its eyes, nibbling broken glass.

Author's Note: If you drive down an unmarked dirt road in Mississippi you may happen upon this mansion. It showed me that houses as well as people can die, in this case slowly, and though old and decrepit, may still retain the imprint of their original beauty.

Sharon Scholl
CANYON DE MUERTE

How nothing ever vanishes completely:
    the waves of some lost
    river still here
    in the crests and ripples
    of its sandy bed.

How universal pain is:
    three hundred Navaho
    mercilessly starving
    on an isolated rock.

How strong the urge for permanence:
    a thousand years
    of petroglyphs insisting,
    "we were here."

How deep our instinct for identity:
    countless outlined
    hands proclaiming
    their particularity.

How brief a time we share:
    here between
    these red rock walls
    tomorrow already
    touching yesterday.

Author's Note: The Navaho reservation area of Arizona records early occupation of North America by humans. It has become a symbol of resistance against European invasion and the willingness of native peoples to die rather than surrender.

Katie Kingston

A SHORT WAY
Las Ruinas de Chichén Itzá

We walk these steps, too narrow
for our feet, too steep for our spirit,
pressing our fingers to gray stone, hand
over hand to steady ourselves against this height.
At the top an altar connects us to ritual,
the heart cut from the body. The stone man,
semi-reclining, still holds the sacrificial tray
now paled white under the same sun. One by one
we touch it trying to absorb the promise
of an exotic god, jaguar or serpent.

And when we don't understand the silence
under our fingers, we step back and take pictures
trying to center the altar between two pillars
that once supported a roof. We read
about the women, their bruised skulls found
in the cenote, pushed over an edge
into the sweet water of this underground river.
It is easy to imagine them piecing together
a thatched roof or rocking children in the cool sling
of a hammock, and later, when the sun was highest,

shooing iguanas from the flat stones
where they placed laundry to dry. It is harder
to imagine them on the stone steps at noon, under a sun
that was god and calendar, praying for rain, giving
children for rain. In our own way, we feel
the same gods inside us, this rationale
for death. We have climbed such a short way
to the top of this pyramid, and we will go down
the same way we came up, lowering our center
of gravity one step at a time, clutching
the cabled rail to steady our descent.

Author's Note: At these ruins in Yucatan, Mexico, I was especially concerned with the lives of the women and their role in the sacrificial rites.

Gladys Swan

JOURNEY TO THE MAYA

I. NIGHT WITH FIREFLIES
(In the courtyard of Uxmal)

If I sing to the stones, don't count me mad.
Or call me mad—just let me sing.
They sing to me, these bones
of the buried past, skulls rising up,
leaves of fire blossoming
from their eyes.
They sing as the stars sing
of light years vanished, never gone—
always saying goodbye,
the ephemeral sings:
Imagine: on a planet
hung like a crystal in space
an eye so keen it sees
galaxies of fireflies twinkling
from the earth.

II. CENOTE
(Dzibilchaltún)

This pool fed by hidden springs
opens to the sky, a mirror—
embraces lilies within a shelf of rock.
The roots of old trees twist to form a seat
where one can pause to study
the patience of water, wait for the pilgrims
to come and dip their hands, touch water
to their brows before they take the road
to the temple of the sun.
How ancient water is, how clear of artiface!
Here the shade, the cooling touch.
Wings—a monarch, green and black,
red dragonflies endlessly mating:
The pool lies open, an eye
to whatever gives it an image of itself:
Clouds and dragonflies, shadows
of lilies, delving roots, dreaming grass.

III. SUN AND MOON
(Palenque)

The sun is on my head and in my lap.
Does it matter? I am well past bearing.
It mounts beyond the populations
antlike on the steps,
sets beyond them too, leaving
the sacred stones to the heave of jungle,
the cries of monkeys—whatever moves
beneath the lunar gaze.

In the temple of the moon
the goddess bears a tree of light,
snakes branching into arms,
wavering like water,
a snake held out in offering.
Above the birth canal a small god
begins to penetrate her womb.
What will she bear, this image
to be reckoned with?

The then lies in the now:
the violence of new birth
beating at the gates.
the heave, the bloody flux
till it slips through and meets
the air, the greater light,
this, the dark womb's creation.

You wanted to dance.

Author's Note: These are selections from a longer cycle. "Night with Fireflies" is set in the quadrangle of the Nunnery Complex, four buildings elaborately carved with masks of the rain god Chac and serpents at the corners. Dzibilchaltún (Place Where There Is Writing On Flat Stones) was a ceremonial center for the Mayas, flourishing from 2000 BC until the Conquest. The cenote was both a water source and a sacrificial well. Palenque in Chiapas, Mexico is renowned for its impressive temples and carvings. The Temple of Inscriptions houses the sarcophagus of the great third century ruler, Lord Pakal.

Margaret Blaker

PACAL'S TOMB

Deep down a claustral flight
of steps far from the light,
stone–faced, remote and tall,
the Nine Lords of the Night
are braced against the wall.

Garments of stucco paste,
jade pendants bleached and white,
their phantom feathers fall
in graceful arcs; and like a pall
drenched in the tears of time,
a crystal limestone curtain covers all.

Author's Note: In Palenque, Mexico the tomb of Pacal, a Maya ruler who died in 683 AD, is deep beneath his pyramid. Ground water seeping from the surrounding limestone bedrock has deposited a semi–transparent veil over the stucco figures on the walls.

Netta Gillespie

MONUMENT: COBA

Breast of stone, once smooth,
stripped now, rib after rib,
to scarred gray bone:
On the crest, a temple, hard
nipple for dead gods to suck,
but fallen now, sliding
like rain down the long
declination. Everywhere,
traces. We are crotch–deep
in bones. Even cliffs
are compelled to recite. Wind
carves monuments. We give
names to these. The dead
retain names for a time.
Scars of wind and grit erase
these. It has nothing to do
with us in our red mittens,
pausing to decipher worn
messages. The dead are strange
to us, their smell, even now,
sweet and forbidding.

Author's Note: This haunting archaeological site in the Mexican state of Quintana Roo is the remains of a town built around shallow lakes, first settled as early as 400 BC. Long before the Spanish arrived, the city's inhabitants died out mysteriously and dense jungle grew over everything.

Michael Gill

NOTES FROM THE INCA TRAIL

I. ALAUSI

Let these be the words
that take you to a place
where the moon radiates

pale silver behind a dark
and stony ridge, and these
be the words to show you

the mountain's inky profile,
a jagged tear of black. No
light glimmers but fireflies

and stars, and only silence
echoes off the valley
walls, around the fireflies,

beneath the constellations.
In solitude above the tree line:
you start walking there.

II. QUILLOLOMA

Sometimes you hear birds
calling like water dripping
question marks in a still pool.

Sometimes you hear birds:
an eerie whistle in the distance.

Sometimes you can hear them
even when they are not calling:
such is the silence.

You hear their still wings brush
the air as they push through it

overhead. Such is the silence:
you stop breathing
to avoid making such a racket.

III. LAGUNA LOS TRES CRUCES

Woman with your mule,
mule hauling sticks
passing a lake

on the stone Inca road,
poncho clad woman
felt hat woman,

barefoot woman
walking,
walking—

if it rains,
well then:
it rains.

Author's Note: Outside the towns, in the Andean sierra of Ecuador, no artificial light penetrates. The Inca trail, still useful hundreds of years after the fall of the Incas, wanders through these mountains. Alausi is a tiny town of stone streets. Where the town vanishes just a block off the square, the trail winds out into the landscape. Quillaloma is a hill surrounded by hills on the sides of the mountains, and Laguna Los Tres Cruces is a pond along the trail.

Maria Quinn

STONES OF THE SACRED VALLEY OF THE INCAS

Here gray stone has usurped a place of prominence,
a status asking more than mere respect. Rock
is sent up out of the ground in *huacas* like
a note, *Mother's thinking of you. Don't forget.*

The Intihuatana tethered the solstice sun with a
golden chain to prevent its gyrating off
to warm a more serviceable world. By it,
Inti was anchored to the sphere of human endeavor.

More clever even than the ancient ones
whose labor engendered their puzzling perfection,
these stones imitate the shapes of mountains
and starless spaces in the Milky Way.

Like the Urubamba before it was altered,
they zigzag to channel chicha and the flow
of llama blood, that the divining
might know the intent of heaven.

One huge boulder, smooth and potent, is ensconced
like a dispenser of dispensations, at the entrance
to the great cathedral, granting its faithful
(or not granting) permission to attend the Mass.

Hewn blocks loom, leviathans,
to protect their people,
turning massive volcanic–stone angles
around corners of their lives.

In walls of the Koricancha they hold hands
in a circle and crouch like children
in a pact of secrecy, concealed first
by gleaming plates of gold, then hiding

beneath a Spanish church till the trembling
earth reveals their unmarred solidarity.
Stone vats for chicha beer to sate the sun's thirst
become baths for shivering friars in the new

and seemingly blasphemous world view.
Some take the shapes of necessary things—
animals, homes,—and offer themselves into the
ground to *pago* Pachamama from whence they came.

Great ones nestle among each other like lovers,
curves and angles as distinctive as the shape
of the only one who fits. They ascend with
ferns and philodendrons of the *selva*

to the saddle between the Picchus, old and new,
become there a city raised aloft as chalice.
What juts up jagged from the ground
is companioned with eased familiarity

by finely finished Inca walls
as if the finest work of earth and man
were meant to stand in timeless conjuction
on an altar between green peaks.

Author's Note: Some of the world's finest masonry is found in Cuzco, Peru and the surrounding regio
culminating at Machu Picchu. The Koricancha, or temple of the sun, was the center of the Inca empire
Its expertly curved walls, once covered with gold, were revealed again in 1950 when an earthqual
destroyed the church which the Spanish conquerors had built over the top of it. The huge stone vess
that once held chicha, a sacred drink offered to the sun god Inti, had been used as a bathtub for cleric

Ruth Moon Kempher

QUIPU SONG, NEAR THE TOP

    "Hiram Bingham counted
three thousand sets of stairs" says Julio.
"We can't go up them all."

    And I murmur thank you
to whatever Gods may listen. I'm not sure
if these terraces count as stairs—deep steps
cut into the earth side, green now with grass
made greener by dew, watered by clouds
that sit easy against the mountain.

              High on Machu Picchu
where eight Inca highways converge below me
like web-strings of stone and trodden earth,
almost up to the top-most platform, I stop to rest.
Behind me is an altar and ahead, blue sky.
And below, in its gorge, by all that's holy,
is Neruda's silver river, slashed by uprisen
teeth of rock, dazzling rapids
of writhing sheen—a shimmering silver
snake of a river, the sacred Urubamba
winds between snow peaks, upcropped
and distant. And beside that river
the powerful orange train hauling tourists
is a toy lost in a world of green.

    "Machu Picchu never was lost,"
Julio tells us, " We never lost it.
But we don't know what they believed."
I think he knows.
They believed in the worth of stones.
They believed in their work and
in this place
which was sacred, concentric.

The top is only top.
I'm seated here, central, by the altar
at the set core of the universe, at this
gathered point of stillness.
Listen to the laughter, the wind rising
against this earth sings in tangles of stone
and highway dust, songs of home trees.
Visiting the gods here, we find
our separate ease.

Author's Note: Machu Picchu is an Inca settlement, high in the Peruvian Andes. Its large areas of agricultural terracing and stone buildings were rediscovered in 1911 by Hiram Bingham. The well-preserved highways and archaeological sites are a testament to the Inca civilization which once flourished there.

Quipu is the name given to the bundled strings, often made of colored cotton, whose clustered knots were an Incan system of record keeping.

Joseph Powell

THE THEATRE OF EPIDAURUS

A coin dropped center-stage
is a principle of acoustics—its echo climbs
each seat, sits on the rim, falls over the edge
into history. We imagine the lines of poets
reaching out like healing hands
to assuage a beautiful dumb boy
whose forehead is anointed with oil,
a hoplite with a spear-wound in his jaw,
a barren woman, kohl-eyed, penitent.

Power was inscribed within belief
like an almond hardening into fruit—
a clear tear fixed on sweetness.

The Sicilians so loved their theatre
only captives who knew Euripides by heart
were spared a bloody death or marble quarries.

Now the poet's words are goat-trails
through pine-covered hills.
Red anemones, more red than all the blood
surgeons let or Hippolytus's twenty horses,
spill their glossy, sunlit cups of color
down the hillsides like words
the chorus chose to exit by.

The quiet here is talkative
so when that coin-drop dies
we're suddenly aware
of the stairs and empty stone seats
that flow like drapery down
to a pool of dust.

Author's Note: Located near Nauplion on the eastern shore of the Peloponnese peninsula, the Theatre of Epidaurus was built in the third century BC. Part of the ancient complex for healing which centered around the worship of Ascelepius, son of Apollo, it is one of the most well-preserved amphitheatres in Greece.

Joseph A. Soldati

AMONG RUINS

—Ancient cities need no maps.

I.

At Tiryns and Mycenae
the cyclopean walls still stand,
yet the wide ways are empty,
their paving stones crenated
like the brains of men.

Texture is important, there is poetry in stone:
the Nemean lion devours a man
and blood runs from the vein;
on a gravestone carving at Delphi
a slave holds mirrors to the sun.

The record is in the rock:
neglect of gods made the volcano erupt,
the earthquake ravage, the invasion overthrow.
Eddies of air swirl through vacant courtyards.

What you brought to your gods has been taken:
in foreign bazaars merchants sell votive figures,
their niches empty in the faded walls
beneath ceilings open to the wingsweep of birds.

II.

Romans, your intimate rooms open for outings,
tourists litter your sleeping places
where nightly you held to warm lovers
while the wind swept the darkness
into piles against the hills.

Where you took dinner and drank
the red wine with great joy,
trees are growing.

And where you came to bathe,
lizards soak in the sun,
mosaics on the gray stone.

Empty, except for cats, the theater waits.
Players' masks laugh and weep
their locutions for ghosts—
an audience enters, an audience departs—
dancers no longer tread from the dark.

Paestum, where roses burn on cold altars,
and wrens nest in the pocked architraves
of temples. Fiesole, where through
three perfect arches, you once measured
the moments of the stars.

III.

The stones proclaim who worked the stone,
yet few signatures remain:
Pythagoras of Samos, Georg of Verona,
Arturo Soldati of Vecciatica—
eloquent epitaphs all their own.

Stone takes its shape in time,
stands to storm, but is pitted by rain,
wears in the air, falls in the flame,
is buried by earth and uncovered again.

Among ruins music is crystalline,
its movements convoluted,
and time's cacophonies suspend.
Touch one ancient column
and know why the stone is fluted:
you can hear it in the wind.

Author's Note: The ruins in the poems are a composite of many ancient sites of Greece and Italy. Sculptors and stone masons have been signing their work in stone since antiquity: Pythagoras at Olympia and Georg in the medieval Church of San Zeno in Verona. Arturo Soldati, my grandfather, learned stone cutting as a youth working on the Simplon tunnel. He signed the house he built in Vecciatica, Italy.

Rina Ferrarelli

PYTHAGORAS ACADEMY

Sun–drenched avenues,
palm trees, oleanders.
Low white buildings,
and a dazzling *lungomare*.
The sand blackish,
the water shallow far into the sea.
On the way over
we saw the sarcophagus
of a general rising in a field,
row after row of melons
lying quietly around him.
And at the cape, the site
where Pythagoras Academy used to be
squared off and numbered
like a multiplication table.
Only one gigantic column remains
of the temples and school.
It towers across the centuries
reaching far above the Ionian sea.

Author's Note: I grew up in southern Italy, thirty miles from Crotone where Pythagoras Academy used to be.

Rina Ferrarelli

ANTINOÜS AND THE CHARIOTEER

We rest in the cool sleek portico
before going in to see what's survived,
fragments that hint at what might've been
a selection of a selection we make the most of
no matter how provisional. Detached
from the full context like a memory,
a deed we wish to be remembered by.
A chipped urn, a frieze, a column
or pediment, at times an entire vase
with time frozen on it, a statue
with only a broken arm, a broken hand,
one of many, or something miraculous:
Antinous, present in every inch
of his young beautiful body.
He knows he's going to live forever,
with or without Hadrian's love,
the sculptor's work. Immanence itself.
As close, as anchored to the ground
as the Charioteer hovers above it.
Horses and chariot missing
he stands there still, feet together,
back straight, slim body gracefully robed,
eyes, like those of the artist, I imagine,
fixed on the invisible goal. Nothing else
exists for him. Neither the swaying chariot,
nor the nervous, snorting horses
rock the quiet of this youth, gathered in himself,
lifted by his passion above everything.

Author's Note: I saw these two statues in a museum in Delphi, Greece. Antinous was purported to have been one of Hadrian's lovers.

Anthony Russell White

MARY'S HOUSE NEAR EPHESUS

"... John took Mother Mary with him."
—John 19:25–27

On Bülbül Mountain
near Ephesus
is the stone house
where Mary lived
after John brought her
at last to safety.
And there the flowing spring
that began so long in the past.
Nearby flourishes an olive tree,
daughter of the fore–mother tree,
which rose from an olive
that slipped one day
from Mary's hand.

Author's Note: St John brought Jesus' mother with him when he went to Ephesus, Turkey. In the 20th Century, a French nun had a vision that brought her to this spot on Bülbül Mountain outside Ephesus where foundations of a house were found. It was then restored and has become an active place of pilgrimage. Ruins of the basilica of St. John are nearby.

Sandy Feinstein

AT THE RUINS OF SAN SIMEON IN SEPTEMBER

Stones climb out of thistle and Saint Simeon's sand
from where his pedestal overlooks the city he didn't see
year after year standing or sleeping cramped,
eyeing his rest in the New Jerusalem.
The lizard slithering down one great column
casts a weak shadow on the wild figs
beyond reach of three grazing horses,
their coats twitching in the hot September sun
beating down on pilgrims wandering this desert
to see something and finding a bloody black bull
gutted, fallen among these Byzantine ruins
and drawing flies as if there were no salvation.

Author's Note: San Simeon in Syria is considered the jewel of the so-called "dead cities." St. Simeon was an ascetic monk who, after various spiritual tests, finally settled in the eponymous place, where he ascended a 16–18 meter high pillar and stayed there for the next 42 years, until his death in 459. Extensive remains of his church, as well as the convents, monasteries, and chapels that were built after his death, make this site one of the most evocative in Syria.

Sandy Feinstein

AIN DARA

Lion claws that might belong to elephants'
dusty gray hides cut from black basalt
leave thick bodies towering over
golden, sandy feet leading or looking

to one footprint that must be god's, big
as the dark hulks left, unlike the delicate
ornamentation, dots like Arabic fives
or zeroes, circled by western ciphers

barely cracked beside the Hittite giant's
flat foot vulnerable in Aramaea's sun
also setting near Afrin's grazing sheep
left unmolested by those great stone paws.

Author's Note: Near Afrin in northern Syria, Ain Dara is another dead city, but considerably older than San Simeon. It is the site of a Hittite temple thought to be from the first millenium B.C. The Aramaeans conquered the Hittites.

Ann Struthers

FOOTPRINTS AT THE TEMPLE AT AIN DARA, SYRIA

Two black basalt lions, once sitting on their haunches,
have been waiting for us so long they've toppled.

"The past is a bucket of ashes," a box of rubble
and stones. The past is the old wind from Macedonia.

In the river valley below an ancient Arab plows his field
with his team of donkeys. Slow in the sun, and slow.

Ishtar stepped upon these stones and the weight
of her glory sunk her footprints in granite.

"Not heaven itself upon the past has power;
what has been has been ..." the dead bury their dead.

Two storks—we can see their black wing tips,
their red legs—circle, searching for updrafts.

The Prophet's pointed shoe printed in limestone at Bosra
and where his dagger rested, it burned its shape.

Holy places and miracles: Halep where Abraham stopped
to milk his cow. The Crusader's icon which weeps holy oil.

The winged sphinxes on this frieze would fly like storks
if they could, the seated lions would get up, stretch, roar.

I would roar, too, not for the past, but for the future
of this desert country where we breathe the dust of the dead.

Author's Note: Japanese archaeologists excavating the temple have put in place a number of the stones carved in bas relief with representations of various animals including winged sphinxes. Legend has it that Abraham stopped in Halep (Aleppo) to milk his cow on his journey south. The crusader icon in a convent near Ma'lula supposedly weeps holy oil. The footprint of Mohammed is in the oldest Mosque in Syria at Bosra.

Sandra Goldsmith

A STREET IN CAIRO

A twelfth century mosque
whispers its cupolas, bejeweled windows;
breathes quietly lest its elegance
show up its neighbor–marketplace
where some people
fast–walk in slow motion
past heaps of trash,
donkey carts, pickup trucks.
Their arms swing as elbows brace
against clusters of merchants
hawking wares.
Others slow–waltz
to a melody of aromas,
their trays of lamb, rice, flatbread
held above the throngs.
Steam rises;
creates one more homage
to the Power above
before families settle into circles
outside their stalls
to share
the Ramadan break–fast meal.
Nearby, a centuries–old minaret
still stands tall,
pays its own respects.

Author's Note: My visit to Egypt, particularly Cairo, brought forth a recurrent theme—that of contrasts: donkey–driven carts alongside cars on main thoroughfares; road– and pedestrian–traffic frenzy giving way periodically to peaceful praying in mosques; desert land on one side of an outlying road and fertile land on the other.

Amy Stewart

ANCIENT EGYPT IS BEHIND YOU

Try to sleep. Just imagine
how quiet, how calm it is
far above the plains of Arabia.
The Libyan Desert is like the sea:
it will try to hold you forever.
It gives up its jewels
only after many centuries.

You have lost nothing coming here.
Your touch is so slight
that it is hardly felt.
A person could spend their days
watching the almond-eyed girls
carry their baskets on the walls
in a long procession,
and send out clouds of pigeons
as they pass.

One need not have any great sorrow
to desire such a life.
Even the conqueror of the world
was not ashamed to admit
that he had been conquered
by a girl of eighteen.
Expect no different of yourself.

You belong to no race on earth.
If you sleep at all, believe
that someday you will awaken,
and the human emotions of men and women
will again exist in this land
of palm and pomegranate.

Author's Note: This poem can loosely be described as a cento, a poem made up of lines from other works. It originated not in Egypt but in Berkeley, California. The title came from a sign in the history section of a bookstore whose shelves had recently been rearranged, and some of the lines came from the dusty old history texts on the shelf, many of them over a hundred years old.

Steve Barfield

AN EGYPTIAN EVENING

In this light the sand is gray
the hibiscus garden wants to escape it
and crowds thirsty around the well.
The emerald date palms drape
a low quarter crescent
of a topaz moon.

From a distant valley
the bark of a lone fox.
But closer is the insistent tapping echo
against a smooth stone wall.

The pyramid tombs are competitors of time
and immense fortresses of forever.
Backlit with the light of the universe
these dark triangles are rigid
with an unbending will.
They press their faces into the infinite.
Yet at one broken corner
is an hourglass leak,
the beginning of their slow subsidence
into the anonymous drifting desert.

Look down into that crack of light
and see the fever of so many oil lamps.
The sound of the loyal priests
is coming from the hidden room.
There are hushed breaths and urgent whispers
and through the funereal smoke
an obsidian glint.

The papyrus scrolls are inscribed
with all that will be needed

Knowing Stones

for a spiritual lifetime
and rolled with a rare incense.
The scarab beetle amulet
is a jeweled fetish of time.

A mummified falcon in a jar
dreams of a soaring sun.

And the walls are relieved
with a multicolored embroidery of mystic embossments.

There is also the sound of the grave robbers
chipping away at the night.
These echoes make their own sense of time
that allows it to decay
geometrically.

Author's Note: I have always been fascinated with the ever-evolving mysteries of early Egypt.

Christopher Conlon

AT THE GREAT ZIMBABWE RUINS

I.

Kings strode here. They looked
below themselves, down the big grassy hills,
to the gleaming black bodies lifting
bits of empire onto their backs—
struggling, bandy–legged under the burden
of the stones, they climbed the trail
of red earth, where others, also shining under
the huge southern sun, waited to lift,
strain, shout instructions, hand one
to the next.

II.

It is a honeycomb sliced open
for the sky to see. Passages
and chambers, paths and turnabouts,
a spiralling construction of circles
leading upward, ever upward,
to a destination which must have been
some kind of heaven. The stones,
ten thousand or more, were cut
with the precision of gems
and placed, one atop another,
in smooth symmetry: it is the grace,
the delicacy that is astonishing.
It took one hundred years.

III.

Seven times that number have passed now,
seven hundred years of suns and darknesses,
of flowerings, wind, and voices.
What is left stands. The rest is
seven centuries' shattered, blasted to oblivion.

Knowing Stones

IV.

This Sunday morning is clear and warm,
almost balmy. I look below myself,
where tourists in t-shirts
are crawling up, like white ants,
toward me. I hear their voices.

I wonder if kings are listening.

Author's Note: Once a thriving city, Great Zimbabwe is known to have been abandoned, apparently hastily, for reasons which remain a mystery. The Ruins are among the oldest standing structures in southern Africa.

Phillis Gershator

WALKING THE WALL

I.

The wall has been renovated
many times over, and the people died
as they do for every tunnel,
for every bridge and dam

Their spirits hang around

Crossing a span, waterway or chasm
we invoke them
and breath a little easier on the other side
though at the end of this climb
I'm not the only one out of breath
Too many spirits on our backs

II.

The stone steps are worn
especially the steepest ones
I cling to the rail
conscious of the wall walkers before me
Their footsteps near the railing
multiplied ten thousand times and more
leave grooves in the stone
where I fit my own
secure in the well trodden path
at the extreme right or left

Knowing Stones

III.

After the south Seventh Tower
where the crumbling core's exposed
teenage barbarians breach the wall
cutting loose
singing yelling climbing over the rocks—
children of a dynasty
falling apart
overdue for renovation.

Author's Note: In China I visited the Great Wall, built by the First Emperor to keep Barbarian warriors from crossing the northern border. The wall is also called the "Wall of Tears" because it contains not only stones and earth, but the bones of those who died constructing it and the tears of those who came looking for their lost or missing loved ones.

William Wei-Yi Marr

THE GREAT WALL

I.
The struggle between civilization
and barbarism
must be ferocious

See this Great Wall
it twists and turns
with no end in sight

II.
What valor
to climb the ragged ridge
and to look long and hard
through a self-adjusting lens
at the skeleton of the dragon
that sprawls miles and miles
in the wasteland
of time

Author's Note: Stretching 4,500 miles, the Great Wall of China was built more than 2,000 years ago to protect an ancient Chinese empire from northern militant tribes that were regarded as barbarian. Standing on the Great Wall for the first time in 1986 with my family, I had a vision of the skeleton of a dragon, an imperial symbol in old China, sprawling over space and time, and moving towards me.

John Calvin Rezmerski
A GIFT OF TWO STONES, FOR MR LIANG

"There was a wall."–Ursula K. Le Guin, *The Disposessed.*

And there was a great lake that spit out agates,
layered pastries that took eons to bake,
hard and multi–hued and delicious to the mind.
Continents and seas have all they need of time,
to eat and digest and compose themselves and sleep
and spit out pretty things for humans to keep.

And the Wall, like all walls and all else
that humans cook up for themselves
thinking of permanence and safety from the new,
sooner or later comes down as all walls do.
And we might keep a fragment or two
to remind us some collapses are overdue.

We human, each by each, have so little time
in which to wait, and only hope for enough life
to see big walls become mere curiosities.
We applaud the fall of our neighbor's walls
and hope our friend's name will be remembered,
that his family, years from now, will recall
that the latest heap of old wall was what he longed
to see, covered over with flowers layered
like an agate disgorged by a great lake,
the agate of a nation's lives, compressed, baked,
multi–hued, ancient, but tasting like open air.

Author's Note: After the Tiananmen Massacre, a Chinese friend spoke of the Great Wall as a symbol of the futility of efforts to stifle knowledge and free speech. On his return to China, I gave him this poem and two stones: a Lake Superior agate to remind him of Minnesota and a fragment of the Berlin Wall as a reminder that no oppression can last forever.

Dale Sprowl

THE WESTERN WALL

Once at the great Western Wall we
wept; that day at the wailing wall,
weeping and wailing for ourselves, our ancestors,
gentile and Jew, there at the wall where we
entered on the women's side,
were required to wear aprons while our friends,
our brothers, went wearing cardboard *yarmulkes*
to the men's side: there we
wept and prayed and prayed and wept and stuffed
scribbled messages to God in the place
between the stone blocks where mortar should be;
into cracks in crumbling bricks we
stuffed our prayers and we
dented our foreheads on the yellow white rock—
impressions that Jew, gentile, old, new,
must wear on their foreheads:
the wounds ... the wounds,
wounds of war, wounds of want, wounds of worry,
wounds within the soul; we
wondered, we
wished, we
pushed our prayers deep
into the wall.
And then, later, outside the wall, we
danced, danced with young men not pretending to be soldiers,
young men who did the *hora* with us,
Uzis bouncing on their backs
as they were not pretending to protect the borders
of their tiny enemy–locked country.
They were not pretending to be soldiers,
they were not pretending to wear Uzis,
they were wearing them,
trained to wear them like we
learn algebra.

All night long after we
danced there
and danced with tambourines on table tops
in a Medieval fortress we
heard the muffled pops of gunshots in Jerusalem.
Oh Jerusalem, oh Jerusalem,
you who kill the prophets and stone those sent to you,
How often I have longed to gather your children together,
as a hen gathers her chicks under her wings,
but you were not willing.
Look, your house is left to you desolate.

Author's Note: Jerusalem is the Holy City for Jews, Christians, and Muslims. The political climate of Israel, coupled with the pilgrims' receptivity to the land as God's country, create an experience of magical realism with a threatening edge. The Western Wall is the only remaining part of the Second Temple, built by Herod and destroyed by Rome under the rule of Titus in 70 AD. It stands as a symbol of Jewish piety, ancestry, and mourning. The end quotation is from the New Testatment, Luke.

Enid Shomer

FROM THE WAILING WALL

It's an ordinary rock
without a single elegant edge,
a dolt of a rock unlike the arrowheads
we've found in streams,
those nimbly chinked blades
that cleave the light with one purpose.
This rock hoards shadows
in its pocked surface.
We place it next to our other books
as if it were the fossil record of prayer,
an unsplit geode with ancient words
glittering at its core.

Soon the bit of rubble rules
the house, paring all our goods
down to mannerisms, ploys.
It is the weed in the garden of history,
what must be swept again and again
from doorsills, the part of the outside
that keeps wanting in. It is the muscle
of the land. If there is another world
this is its scaffolding—what comes to hand
from the hard earth for building
or throwing under our blue
curfew, the sky.

Author's Note: Located in Jerusalem, the Wailing Wall was not part of Israel until after the Six Day War in 1967. Jews pray and conduct religious ceremonies at the Wall. Some leave prayers on paper wedged between the stones.

Elisavietta Ritchie

READING THE STONES

I watch for rocks
to guide me along
perilous journeys:

a configuration
of balanced boulders
on a cliff above
dangerous straits,

inukshuit, humanoid
cairns created by ancient
Arctic peoples to mark
a way through blizzards,

or a certain shape
of granite ridge
silhouetted against
the carnelian sun,

a natural heap
of debris spilled
by an avalanche

warning: beware
gravelly slopes
and trying to climb
too high.

On a cold beach
I inspect
scatterings of stones,
try to decipher

jasper and agate,
quartz shot through
with serpentine,

glassy obsidian,
and speckled pebbles
glistening with mica.

I pocket the gray
stone ringed with
a perfect white circle.

Author's Note: The *inukshuit* cairns are still used by the Innuit today. I sift through stones as well as shells on the beaches of the world.

Love Among the Ruins

It is love that calls us into life, onto the road of this great adventure, and love that sends us off with our last breath into the great unknown. No wonder our ideas of travel are strangely interwoven with thoughts of love. One plans an itinerary with it; another hopes to meet up with it on the way. Some search out breathtaking panoramas to share with it; others expect the trip to bring it about, enhance it, revive it, or allow them to forget it.

How often the adventures of young lovers, not only draw them together, but define the nature of the relationship they are building as they get to know the world. But we will also see that there are limitations to the degree a vista can re-enliven what is dying.

The traveler, embarking on love as on any adventure, can never anticipate what form it will take. For love itself is as unpredictable as the trains and buses without schedules in remote places.

W. K. Buckley

STONE LEMONS

    The hike up is steep,
      from Oaxaca.
The Mexican sun a medallion,
      and on hills old *viejitas* build their fires,
      small ones, flaming close to living holes.

    I remember the approach:
      as strangers to ceremonies,
        cleft by the ghosts,
      blood moving toward walls
      in a cold breath of order.

High on that mountain
the stone mud pies of a god
      dead–feathered souls
        wavering in chambers, like webs.

    I remember the wind:
      heavy, carving in the ruin,
      moving in our clothes.

Then down into the open court
and my White Heart contracts.

    It was the light:
      bluing the cotton of her blouse,
      covering her arms with chestnut,
      darkening her eyes,
        before Cortez and the slaughter of gold.

No *corridos* here, only the whisper
      of drums, of brown feet in the dust,
        the feathered wind, dancing,
      fanning into masonry,
into the clicks of her beaded anklets.

The sun calls on Monte Albán,
and we carry the woven *mantas*.
    On old ground we bend
      like blades against walls:
    Zapotec stones of *el danzante*.

Sandunga winds spread the skirt
      into the feather–fold of mystery,
      into the stone flesh and clay blood;

and my mouth into the neck of lemon,
into the shoulders of lemon.
Her belt loosening thick smell
of Nahuatlan leather,
      letting go folds of blue cotton blouse,
      its white embroidered flowers
      opening, nestling,
the maize smell of clean market–cloth.

She holds me against the engravings,
against that carefully placed stone,
    with its smell of sun,
and silver–cold
are the stars of altar and knife.

      "La brisa es mia," she whispers.

this
      lemoned in body,
    leathered in the brain.

in the cold stone of lemon.

Author's Note: Above Oaxaca, Mexico, in the mountain–top Zapotec ruin of Monte Albán, the wind moved through her skirt as if she were a dancer. Behind us was the wall of *danzantes*, huge agile figures etched into stone—dancers from a lost era with some unknown inspiration for movement.

Jody Bolz

FIRST CROSSING

for Hugh

Twenty years ago, you woke me
in a hut near Brujenkhola
reeking smoky thatch and goat dung.
Beyond the unglazed window,

full night in the valley floor,
featureless, obscure—
but you pointed to the sky.
Your shoulder pressed mine.

A triangle of coral light
hovered in the blue–black dark:
the mountain
we'd walked days to see,

fish–tailed Machha Puchhare,
flaring like a sun
an hour before dawn.
We lay on our bedrolls,

awake, watching the light grow.
Later, after clay–red tea,
we gathered up our packs,
paid our host and said goodbye.

The inn–keeper's deaf daughter
waved, chasing her sister,
as we started for the river.
Ten minutes to a narrow bridge

across the Seti Khola,
wooden slats half rotted—
cables frayed, too far apart
to grab with our arms out.

We had to walk a line of boards
nailed loosely down the center,
bisecting our vision
of pale–green glacial water

in its bed of chalky boulders
more than twenty feet below us.
You tapped your toe
against each plank

and made your way across,
agile as a gymnast,
hands see–sawing for balance.
After heart–stopping seconds,

you yelled above the rapids' roar,
Wait there, and dropped your pack.
Faster, you retraced your steps
to bring me back,

coaxing from three yards ahead,
Take a step—
now take another.
Don't look at the river.

Head throbbing,
I stepped staring
at the battered boots
that moved in jerks

above the milky current:
one foot, then the other,
stepped—and stepped again—
until I stepped on land!

We shouted and kissed there,
laughing as we sprawled on shore
guzzling water,
brown and iodine–bitter.

Soon we were singing,
climbing the stony track
through thick rhododendron,
juniper, yew.

By noon, dry and dizzy,
we trudged into a clearing
where an angel was waiting
in a whorl of dusty sunlight.

Poised on the ridgeline,
a shirtless boy, eight or nine—
beautiful despite one blind–blue eye—
held out a bowl of oranges

Suntalla, sahib?
and they glowed like gold.
We bought as many as he'd sell,
tore away the bitter skins

with stinging fingertips.
Back to back
in the shade of a banyan,
we sat eating oranges

as if nothing could harm us,
no crossing ever part us.

Author's Note: In the mid 70s, Brujenkhola was a cluster of huts about a day's walk off the Jomosom trek in northern Nepal—a route that begins in Pokhara and carries hikers toward the Annapurna massif of the Himalayas. The village offers a spectacular view of twin-peaked Machha Puchhare, a sacred mountain that was then off limits to climbers.

Darrell g.h. Schramm

EILEEN MUNDA

In September, when what coursed between us
seemed a current we were afraid to wade,
the island called to our eyes
from Loch Leven. Its one wall,
broken, motioned from the mound.
We walked on slabs of shoreline slate
to be closer to the sacred grounds
and across the water saw
angled in grass beneath boughs
the stones of seventh century graves.
Tombstones and ruins. They pull us
to them as though we hear them cry
to be remembered, the way the hungry
tapeworm heart keeps crying to be loved.

Walking back a different way,
you discovered them, the season's last
blackberries. We packed them into our mouths
as we mumbled and clucked in gusto.
It seemed we had no time to lose.
Eileen Munda behind us and the fruit in our hands
bridged us into sweet communion,
applauding our tongues, our hunger to be one.

Author's Note: In the Scottish Highlands of Glencoe floats a tiny, ancient island held to be sacred and off-limits to all but the one or two families, dating back to the 7th century, who are allowed to bury their dead there near the ruins of an old church.

Leza Lowitz

RISING AND FALLING

Along the graves at Pere Lachaise
Conversation is always an approximation of desire.

You wear a coffee stain on a white shirt and she says:
I want to be like that: a language everyone understands

Of pain and embarrassment, but really
Of fallibility.

In Paris the bums are vaudevillian: "I'm Bob Hope's brother
No Hope," "Johnny Cash's cousin No Cash."

You laugh and give them money
Because they ask in such a way as not to ask.

Kundera said it was easy to hold the illusion of love for someone
You never saw,

Hard to keep the one you saw every morning when you woke
From sleep, hearing the city—women opening their

Back doors sliding metal milk crates across porches,
Scratchy as cat's tongues,

The thud of newspapers hitting cement,
The occasional horn from a factory across the Quay,

Industry turning its wheels inside itself
Like an empty drumbeat

Dancing next to your face—
That was the person you worked to love.

You could forgive the crumbs of bread still in her bangs
Or the way she fell asleep with Rimbaud and her mouth open,

Marveling at The Foolish Virgin
And The Infernal Bridegroom.

Somehow your eyes too became more lost than ever
When you looked at her,

Because you imagined in that moment
Asking her to dance, brushing a moth from her shoulder,

Remembering the crepe de Chine
Against her thigh

Was the nightgown her mother had worn after
Giving birth to her.

And even now in the cemetery
Kissing the gentle flutter of her skirt against her thigh

You laugh at your own romantic impulse to
Create something soft when

All around you is
Marble and granite and gravestone.

After the dark restaurant,
Where the green tiled floor rusted

Around its edges while you ate
Escargot, dropping the

Snail whose six babies spilled out curled-up like
Commas bereft of words to complete them,

After this you remember
The orange–haired waitress bringing you coffee

And spilling it on your shirt,
Both of you laughing.

How you knew that time
Had not corrupted her at all,

Not at all,
And that she needed nothing of you,

Like the milkman picking up the empty bottles from
Crowded back porches, she asked only that you

Remember this moment and try to keep it whole.
But you knew the impossible chore of your whole life

Lay in front of you,
Both absent and present at the same time

And you knew that Brongniart built Pere Lachaise
On ground that rose and fell,

Knowing Stones

And you never wanted to be tamed
And you never wanted to grow old,

So when she laughed you imagined everyone,
Colette and Chopin and Moliere and Proust and Balzac

Even the nameless rebels shot against the Federalist's Wall—
Dancing here with you now.

Author's Note: Every aspiring writer dreams of making a pilgrimage to Paris. I was 21 when that dream came true for me. Like many, I ended up in Pere Lachaise, the cemetery on the outskirts of Paris, summoning the spirits of those writers, wanting to believe that great art and great love were possible.

Richard Beban

FIRST ANNIVERSARY PANTOUM

for Kaaren

To the south, the west, amethyst enamel clouds
& lacquered sky. Worlds away, men sweep the Plaka, empty
torrents of gray water—rivers live a moment, reflect on
cobblestones made dark by countless pilgrim feet

& lacquered sky. Worlds away, men sweep the Plaka. Empty
of self we stare at the fading rose shimmer of sun &
cobblestones made dark by countless pilgrim feet,
the coming night. We see beauty & imagine grace

of self. We stare at the fading rose shimmer of sun &,
pouring off your face, reflected light; I celebrate
the coming night. We see beauty & imagine grace
in our vow to the gods, in our human works.

Pouring off your face, reflected light. I celebrate
how we stood & promised in their sight, forever
in our vow to the gods, in our human works,
in Delphic chasms, in stones, in each other's eyes.

How we stood & promised in their sight, forever
& pledged love at once so fragile & so strong
in Delphic chasms, in stones, in each other's eyes.
We have not wavered, though we have trembled

& pledged love at once so fragile & so strong
it holds us close & supports our work—
we have not wavered, though we have trembled
at creation; we are novices, seek the gods' blessing

Knowing Stones

       it holds us close & supports our work—
       to bring the gods to life again—
       at creation we are novices, seek the gods' blessing,
       promise fidelity in all lives, through all

       torrents of gray water. Rivers live a moment, reflect on
       to the south, the west, amethyst enamel clouds.

Author's Note: My wife, Kaaren Kitchell, and I were married in Crete in 1997, after a pilgrimage to the sacred Greek sites like Delphi. Our ceremony included a ritual of our own devising in which we spoke our vows to a circle of the 12 Olympian gods, represented by our twelve wedding guests. We teach a course called "Living Mythically" that attempts to revivify the Greek gods as mentors in our students' lives. The Plaka is the old section of the city of Athens.

Michael Waters

THE LOST CIVILIZATION

for Robin

The lovers are sleeping on shorn sea–cliffs,
their balconies overlooking the black caldera
and those gaudy cruise–ships, toys in the harbor,
where lovers are sleeping in beds below water,

while below them the lovers–turned–stone are sleeping,
sifting through strata of alluvial beds, their
romance long–lasting, dead and living embracing
from the planet's amphora to the stars' milky hair—

while we wander the island at this odd hour,
the broken labyrinths and sandal–worn stairs
ghost–lit in the moon's diminishing aura,
kindling within us unspoken desire:

the missing, Minoan, night–flowing mirror,
the laval, erotic, God–showering fire.

Author's Note: There is evidence to suggest that Thira, more commonly known today as Santorini, the most dramatic Greek island in the Aegean, may have been the site of Atlantis.

Richard Beban

IN INDIA THE STONE TEMPLE GODS

act much like people
in love. They enfold each other
in postures of grace, unashamed
yoni & lingam,
round at breast & thigh, couple
after couple in emulation of stork
& snake & jasmine vine. Their eyebrows arched
like their supple
spines, nostrils full
of the scent of the beloved,
lips full can speak
no other words but the murmur
of corpuscle & membrane
flushed with bliss. Their biscuit skin
rouged at cheek & forehead, their eyes
evolved beyond pupil & iris, reflect
the secret seen at the moment
of remembering
why we were all arranged
in this immortal frieze.

Come, my wife, teach me again how to act
as gods, turn to golden stone
& bliss.

Author's Note: Temple frieze at Khajuraho, India.

Diane Lutovich

FLESH AND SPIRIT

Mogul invaders called the temple carvings
satanic.
The British called them "love temples,"
kept their ladies away.

But it is not their humping and thrumping,
riding and sucking that makes me
want to rip off my clothes,
dive into a warm fleshed man, but

that they're having such fun.

Erotic is not about
position,
it's about pleasure

about the way she fondles his eyes
with her eyes, her mouth
ripening into a half smile
the way he holds her breast like a golden bird.

Looking at hundreds of bodies
carved from one piece of stone,
joined without friction,

it's easy to wear the inside of your body
outside—relive all moments when
flesh and spirit join:
flying off the high board so the body,
like a gull,
slices the water in two.

Easy enough to worship the universe
in the midst of bodies,
curling like vines
around, into each other.

Author's Note: While flying between Delhi and Varanasi, our plane developed engine trouble in Khajuraho. We had five serendipitous hours to explore the temples we had wanted to see.

Michael Waters

PASSION CONCH

No sun today, the rainy
    season barely begun, so
        we sleep late before

performing the instinctive,
    casual, tourists' ritual:
        combing the beach

in search of the unusual
    among the wrack and weedy
        debris. Ahead of me,

you scan the tide–
    line for what remains,
        the left–behind, the false

and glittering sapphires
    the salt's slow churning
        has tossed ashore—

and pull up a shell
    still filled with muscle,
        purple with black

stitching, the heart's
    colors, pulsing:
        Passion Conch:

slug that has journeyed
    farther than we have,
        from silences deeper

than sleep, withstood
    pressure beyond weather,
        seining the forgotten,

prophetic psalms of the sea—
    all ear, or tongue,
        or one foot

probing, till arriving
    here, in your hand,
        object of our naming:

Passion Conch: tight knot
    of spongy knowledge,
        scholar of coral

passages, blind traveller
    absorbing the world:
        salt water, green

minutiae, perhaps two lovers
    biding time in the gray
        light, in light

rain, turning their deep
    desire over and over,
        having finally found,

in the foreign face,
    in the blunt, breathing
        body, a kindred

race, the source
    of flame, a gift,
        a name.

Author's Note: Hua Hin is located on the southeastern coast of Thailand.

Andrew Epstein
CARRY HOME WHAT YOU CAN

> "Crack a rock (what's a thousand years!) and send it crashing among the oaks. Wind a pine tree in a grey-worm's net and play it for a trout; oh—but the moon does that! No, summer has gone down the other side of the mountain. Carry home what we can." —Willam Carlos Williams, *Kora in Hell.*

The coral reef and dolphinfish and mango chutney sunsets
that reorganize mental avenues to beaches.
Soft distant beating, waves, drums,
drone over whatever we can't forget.
We go into each other, like seeds and soil, nut and fruit.

Perfection is an island surrounded by miles of pounding
surf that rises and swells and ebbs as consequences occur,
and it stakes its claim always in a forever embattled place.
Leaf shadows make mazy patterns in the sand, and the
waterfall of pressing plans sends its spray as far as it can.
Where the little outhouse was guarded by a six inch lizard,
a green wedge of scales, patiently watching you,
unblinking blank eye fixed, throat beating,
as you peeled wet bathing suit off chilled skin of your
legs, slid dry shorts into place over your precious middle.

I wait far off in the future at the keyboard, troll the
blue space hanging over that strange, warm moment,
and try to hold whatever is there in the cascade spray.
Little did you know as you lay naked in bed between
crisp sheets that night, the hum and tingle of whatever follows,
the place that mango day would claim.
How could you see me then in a late green afternoon
above the avenues, with my watercolor words before me.
Sliding up the coast, we trail a silver finger along the
island's slender side, in and out of coves,
with the wake of a small boat.
Masks on, we scan the coralscape of shelves, eddies
of drifting leaves waving a wordless hello,
flashing purple wedges turning into fish,
and carry home what we can.

Author's Note: The Caribbean island of Grenada is known for the lush tropical beauty of its white beaches, mountains, rainforest, and spice plantations.

Kelly Cherry

AT NIGHT YOUR MOUTH

At night your mouth moved over me
Like a fox over the earth, skimming
Light and low over the rising surfaces of my body,
Hugging the horizon against hunters;
Or like the other hunted, the one who runs
Back exposed like a billboard to the barbed wire and starved dogs,
The men in guard towers, danger sweeping the snow–patched yard
Every thirty seconds, the shirt you tore,
To make a tourniquet for your leg, fluttering like a signpost
Against the branch of a birch tree, saying THIS WAY:
You were looking for someplace to hide, to crawl into,
A place to lie down in and breathe
Or not–breathe until the dogs pulled the hunters past,
Fooled by water, wind, snow, or sheer luck,
And I folded myself around you like a hill and a valley,
And the stars in my hair shone only for you,
Combed into cold blue and deep red lights,
And the river ran warm as blood under its lid of ice,
And my throat was like an eel pulsing between your palms,
And the air in my blood was tropical, I caught my breath
And held it between my teeth for you
To eat like a root,
There were black grouse in the forest
And the moon on the snow was as gold as your skin
As I remember it shining on Nightingale Lane,
But the dogs' barking in the distance carried too clearly,
A man snapped, STAT!
And you trembled, troubled and impassioned,
You covered your eyes with your hand,
And I felt the shudder slam like the sea
Pummeled by God's fist,
Wind–bit waves sizzling against the fiery cliffs of Liepaja—
And you were the ship
The harbor dreams of, the brave husband
The bride awaits, the seed
For which the earth has prepared itself with minerals and salts,

And I folded myself around you like a windrow and a furrow,
And whispered, so no one, not dog or man or man–dog, would
  overhear: *Now Now now now*
Escape into me.

Author's Note: Latvia, one of three Baltic countries seized by the USSR, is now an independent nation with a parliament. In 1986, when I visited my then-fiancé, Imants Kalnin, a composer and, now, member of the Latvian Parliament, we were trailed by the KGB.

Elliot Richman
THE KISS

> "I see myself again, skin rotted with mud and pest, worms in my armpits, lying among strangers without age, without feeling ... I might have died there ...."
> –Arthur Rimbaud, *A Season in Hell.*

When all I had was my nineteen years
and not even that because
my core belonged to the Corps
as well as the pack on my back and my weapon,

when all I possessed was emptiness
and a copy of *A Season in Hell,*
a present from my high school French teacher
after she heard I was going to Nam,

when all I owned was death,
my squad ambushed three gooks
cooking rice under triple canopy,
killing the two men outright,
the woman gut shot,
her legs torn off by my grenade,
body squirming in silence like a slug
in blood slime,
limbless hips undulating
in mocking love.
"Kill the bitch," the sergeant shouted
as I bent over, about to shoot her
up with all five ampules of morphine,
even though she'd be dead in seconds.

Flinging her head side to side,
long black hair raining
across a photograph—
a young man and woman,
a pagoda and lake in the background.

Knowing Stones

Raising one bloody arm,
two of the fingers missing,
she looked up at me
and whispered in French,
"Kiss me. Kiss me."

And I was the young man in the photograph,
near the Red Pagoda
by the West Lake in Hanoi,
both of us slightly tipsy
after drinking beer,
and eating peanuts
purchased from the old women
outside the open air restaurants,
both of us longing
to make love again in the hotel
on the street of the flower sellers,
the smell of jasmine and roses
soaked into frayed curtains.

And I kissed her open mouth
with the taste of blood
and fish sauce
and I could swear
that her breath smelled
of jasmine and roses
as she died in my arms
in that hotel in Hanoi.

Author's Note: The poem would probably not have been summoned if I hadn't backpacked to Hanoi in the summmer of 1993, part of the time a guest of the Hanoi Writers' Union.

Susan Terris

SHADOWS OF MOREMI

Bush shadows stencil the tent, and the woman
lies supine on the cot eyeing them.
Outside, midday heat devours the air,
and light and shadow are deadened.

For an instant, even the cape doves
suspend their song. The woman stirs.
She fingers her nipples then drops
her hands to the iron bedrail.
She waits for Hemingway, for Finch–Hatton
to appear, discard topee and boots,
sponge her with water from the Okavango.
But languor spreads a paralysis
that stifles lust, so she shifts on the cot,
stares at the outline of a single leaf
and listens to the mad laughter of lourie–birds.

Later, when the Southern Cross burns the sky,
she stands barefoot
under the bowl of night, gazing
and drinking deep in the shadows.

Author's Note: During siesta time one hot afternoon when I was tent–camping in Botswana, having listened to my guide's stories of a lifetime spent tracking game across Africa, I began thinking of what it was like to be a character in an Isak Dinesen story.

Jacqueline Kudler

THE DAY WE SAW THE ELEPHANT

The road was dusty along the high plain,
the driver leading us in a silent
choreography—rolling, unrolling windows
as trucks rose, fell behind us in brown

billows. The air was heavy in the back
seat. Heat, fatigue, the hundred nattering
irritations of the long-married, hung
over, between us like mosquito netting,

smothering any inclination toward
talk. We must have dozed after
the last village, then jolted awake,
stopped suddenly in a forest

of acacia, the driver intoning: Look,
look here! And there he was before us—
a bull, not fully grown, tusks just
brushing the lower branches, ears fanned

out like two great sails, filling,
emptying the afternoon breeze. Holding
us a moment in his heavy-lidded gaze,
he paused, then continued teeing up

the new grass in a gesture elegant
as a soft shoe—small flick of the left
foot, tip up from trunk to hidden
grin, and I loved you again there

in an instant, and the afternoon was
a sudden lace of light in the acacia.

Author's Note: We traveled all day from Nairobi, Kenya to Lake Manyara Reserve in Tanzania over long dusty roads. Just before our first night's camp at Masi Moto, we saw the elephant.

William Greenway

AT ARTHUR'S STONE

They say on simmer dim this stone will stand
then walk the long slope down to Burry to drink.
At the winter solstice, hand–in–hand

for now, the truce between us holding for a while,
we walk the frosted rusty red
of autumn fern, past a moldering pile

of wild Welsh pony bones
to see the grave of an early king,
a stone balanced long ago on other stones.

We touch its blotched gray flank
as millions have, for luck,
as though solidity and poise, its blank

face, could cure us of our yearnings, keep
our lives together till we die.
Nearby's a cairn of those like us, a heap

of stones too numerous to name, too small
to walk, that marks the grave of men
who dragged or sailed it here to rest on tall

and humpbacked Cefn Bryn, to overlook the bay
of cockle sands that glisten when the tide is out,
and be the shrine of girls who came to lay

milk-soaked honey cake upon the ground
before this altar stone,
and crawl three times around,

and if her love were true he would appear,
transported from whatever distant place,
easing through the mist to meet her here.

Knowing Stones

The moon comes up behind a pony white
as a unicorn, the sun goes down
and pinks the sky and bay before the night

recalls this postcard from the past.
Too far away to see the cars
and houses with their shipwreck masts

of washing poles and satellite dishes,
we might be a pelted pair of ancient,
shivering, short-lived, walking wishes

staring at the mound where we will lie.
And every longest day, the sun
will squint between the lids of sea and sky

that never close, and from this height—
as we dream our centuries of thirst
through the long and dying light—

like a mote in an eye that cannot blink,
the stone of one who lost his love
will walk to the sea to drink.

Author's Note: Wales is covered with cairns and dolmens which Celtic and pre-Celtic peoples believed to embody the spirit of a place. Arthur's Stone, the cairn of royalty, is near the stone burial mound of the common people.

Enid Shomer

IN THE VIENNESE STYLE

In the Cafe Imperial, they are bringing out
the Mozart cake with its delicate

pistachio creme. I've been watching the linden
leaves as the wind lifts them

into the streetlights, how they blanch, then darken
as if they are having an argument

with the tree. On the Ringstrasse, trams
wheeze past and lines of home–

bound traffic blur to faint septic streaks.
The scrolls and curves of the Baroque—

lush, gold–leafed, excessive—look like nothing now
to me but hearts stretched out

of shape, the way tonight the soloist
took music plucked on strings and twisted it

through brass. We had a happy week in perhaps
the only city where we could feel

our marriage healed when actually it was forsaken,
utterly lost, when actually it came

to this: we could agree on what was beautiful,
that was all.

Author's Note: Vienna, Austria is known for its elaborate Baroque or "anti–Reformation" art. The circular moat which once defended the city was converted into the boulevard "Ringstrasse" in the nineteenth century.

Kathleen Iddings

TAORMINA, SICILY

In each Italian–leather woman
   scooping endless olives
   from olive grove prisons
   I see my mother, myself,
     stoic and accepting.

In piazza orange trees
   Christmas lights blink;
   old cappuccino eyes
     drink young beauties.

Shops display strawberries
   red as cheeks of Taormina girls
   singing Silent Night in five languages
     Your hand in mine tinsel cold,

Cold as I in our Rome apartment,
   alone on Christmas Eve.
   I light the last match to our marriage—
     join you on a silent train to Taormina.

In the crumbling Greek theater,
   old as Aristophanes, I long
   to create a better drama for us.
     Mount Etna steams in the distance.

The key to joy wound tight this last day,
   tour books spiral us to Castellammare del Golfo.
   Ecstatic, I pirouette the mountaintop view.
     A nearby fortress stands guard.

With an angry blast of your horn
   I'm crammed back in the marriage box.
   Mount Etna hisses in the distance.
     Clawing at the lid, I plan escape.

Author's Note: Residing in Rome in 1979, I went with my husband (now ex) to Taormina, once Churchill's winter playground, for a Christmas that would be extraordinary, and it proved to be just that.

Dale Sprowl

THE TRAIN RIDE TO MOSCOW

It all seemed so friendly at first,
rushing to spend our last *coupones* on *limonade* and Bulgarian
red wine at the station at evening rush hour.
The soot of the station could not mask its
moving blacks and grays—acrylic sweaters, dark suits
and the toothless or silver-toothed men of Kiev.

Before the train pulled out, we took pictures in our tall fur hats.
At home, I still have the mink one, the one Grandma Hilda wore.
In our sleeper, two bench beds with a table welcomed us.
We laughed at the metal toilet at the end of our first class car
and discussed the advantages of being male
under the circumstances.

Later, the porter brought us tea from the large unadorned samovar
near his small cabin, and we warmed ourselves drinking
from glass cups held by filigreed silver bases.
Even the teenage border guards in full uniform
seemed almost friendly.

But as night came, the forest, evergreen, endless,
became ever black.
On and on and I on my small bench, you above me,
your body blue in the cockroach light,
a Karamazov man;
the shrank, shrank, shrank of metal rails,
and I, so frightened, so far away.

Author's Note: With the dissolution of the USSR in 1991, Kiev became the capital of the independent Ukraine. The distance by train to Moscow is over 400 miles, a full night's travel.

Carolyne Wright

THE CONJURE WOMAN

She blows on the crystal ball,
tells me I can have anything.
Hibiscus flowers.
Jacarandá wood charms.
A powder from the Mercado Modelo
that drives men wild.

In the waiting room, the man I want
drums his fingers, makes eyes
at the honey-colored woman
stirring something in the kitchen.
Strands of blue pearls,
passion flower *lenço* on her head.
A little *samba* on the red floor tiles.
Yemanjá, sea goddess,
smiles and waves her fish tail
from the poster on the wall.

The conjure woman turns her wedding rings
around a long story about the sea.
Bahia dialect—the hushed syllables,
palm trees reflecting
on the water, whole sentences
I want to understand.

Samba school drums at the corners,
cachaça bottles passed around.
Women singing the Carnival tune
Não Se Esqueça De Mim.
Don't leave me, don't forget.
My future–full of missing words,
eavesdropping at the tables
of the deaf, late afternoon
smell of exhaustion.

He's gone. Lady Yemanjá laughs
in the room above the kitchen.
I cross the conjure woman's palm
and go out. The whole town
is in the streets, masked dancers
drumming their true names
from continents that still would fit

together—embracing face to face
like lovers in the salt and sweat
of their sea–displacing passion.
Fishermen drag in their nets
and fall to their knees between
the silver thighs of women.

Author's Note: In Salvador, Bahia, in *Candomblé,* the religion which originated in West Africa, deities have acquired counterparts among Catholic saints. Yemanjá, the mermaid–like goddess of the sea and of Bahia's many fishermen, is honored on February 2nd with net–pulling ceremonies, drinking, and dancing. Festivities often overlap with Carnival.

Douglas W. Lawder

TRANSLATING LOURDES

Lourdes at work in the bank,
a pavilion of black marble:
phone at each ear,
another ringing at her desk.
Voices come mixed with water,
she says. Paper money comes muttering.
She's one generation from
a stick shack in the jungle.

Tonight, when the power goes off
like a slammed door all
over the island, her array
of candles lights up the circus-
colored room like a festive shrine.
Her eyes in candlelight go
from bright black to cinnamon,
and her small hands weave the air
quick as swallows as if *they'd*
tracked down the words,
person, tense,
ordered and knotted them all
together into perfect English.

I wake at 3 a.m. when the light leaps
on again. The half–translated
New York Times is a blizzard
of loose pages around the bed.
I hear her mutter scraps of Mayan
in her sleep. She still
grips my hand. Over what precarious bridge
does she want to be led? Outside,
a tropical moon, large and round
as a manhole cover, is spiked
on a palm tree,
and all around us phosphorescent
wetlight rings up on shore
like millions of TVs left on all night.

Author's Note: Cozumel was originally called "Ah Cuzamil Peten," Land of the Swallows, by the Maya. Living there, I met an attractive Maya woman named Lourdes at the bank, and soon realized that her intelligence and efficiency kept the bank operating. I began teaching her English and found her to be an adept student. As I envisioned where her English skills might take her, I wondered how much of her Maya heritage she would have to sacrifice.

Rose Rosberg

PRESAGE AT MACHU PICCHU

Pigmy to the black peaks of mountains,
roofless walls
                hung by their fingernails
                over edging chasms;
mock windows stare out
of this skeleton city.

Only these dawn lovers wander,
through each other, not through ruins.
blind to that grassy street
showing them
                a sundial's broken finger.

They tremble
           with surmise
                      on the brink
of their own surprise
                abysses:
but they know themselves immune,
        ignore
        these scribblings on the air.

How can April lovers believe
that in a brown November
                they may turn tourists
                in their passion's toothless city
straddling
a lost site?

Editor's Note: Ruins of a moutain–top Incan city near Cuzco, Peru.

Maria Quinn

MACHU PICCHU, RAINY SEASON

Of our last hour at Machu Picchu
we won't forego a moment.
Afternoon rains come in from the east,
at first a light mist as we sit on terraces seeing
variegated jungle greens intensifying in diffused light,
a double rainbow arching itself
across the matronly girth of Putacusi.
But we want to touch again smooth remembrance
of the *intihuatana,* to stand a last time
in the geometry of massive stones.
Now it's coming harder and we press
against the south side of walls,
absorbing their warmth, shielded
from the blowing skrim of water
the surrounding jungle is sucking up
like sun. Now it is running in the
water temple, through canals and stone drainage.
Our wind-breakers and shoes soaked through,
we are height-giddy with delight.
Others have found cover or gone
down to the baths of Aguas Calientes.
The water now seems a strong and worthy
companion to stone, an element to be reckoned with.
Higher, wilder, wetter than we have ever been,
we look back at Huayna Picchu, greener than life,
drenched in the waters of heaven,
all the gray stone turning black in the torrent,
a *sonrisa* moon smiling in a darkening sky,
and the Southern Cross above Salcantay
flickering benediction on our being there.

We are unaware, nor would it make us careful to know,
that the rains have washed trees and boulders
onto the tracks and we will spend the night
below shapely holes in the Milky Way,
wet clothes turned cold in night air of Andean heights,
packed like *despacho* packets of a *pago,*
into the second class car of the last train for Cuzco
on separate seats so only my eyes can reach you,
cold, wet, and blessed to the bone,
with November rains of Machu Picchu.

Author's Note: Sometimes a shared discomfort in a place of great beauty can be love's unexpected ally. *Despacho* and *pago* both refer to offerings to *Pachamama* or Earth Mother.

Elliot Richman

WILL YOU TAKE ME INTO DEATH WITH YOU

Late in Florida light,
an artificial lake,
a room glutted with
grandchildren,
an arid husband,
the indifferent son,
machines to forestall
the inevitable
liquefaction,
will you remember
my dissolute lips?

As a nurse grips
your wrinkled pulse,
will his fingers
feel like El Greco's
as we made love
in our room across
from the Prado,
your husband fishing
in the states,
or will they singe
like the sun
on the nude beach
in Sagres,
hair dousing
my shoulders,
as I squat,
smoking a Gaulois
and peeling an orange
with a switchblade,
while you jump
an imaginary rope
in the surf,

Knowing Stones

in the same ocean
as your husband's
hook, me for once
so glad to be alive,
my whole body
comes inside you,
as you beckon for
me to join you
in the water.

Author's Note: Sagres, Portugal was called in the middle ages "the end of the world" because of its location at the southeastern extreme tip of Europe. I was alone in Sagres in the summmer of 1992.

Kelly Cherry

PLANS FOR A HOUSE IN LATVIA

In a basket on the sideboard,
pile ripe apples;
when the sun reaches them through the open door,
we'll have fire for food.

In fine weather, you write music out back—
or steal off.
"Good fishing among birches and pines!"

In the winter, we skate
on the lake in the field,
and come in late,
blowing on our hands.

Silence falls on the little house,
sticking like snow all around,
the only sound your voice,
startling and mysterious
as the shadow of a blue spruce
cast across cold ground.

At night, Princess leaps from the wood floor
to the chair where she sleeps,
while we share the big bed.

Your warm body covers mine like a blanket.

Dear heart,
a final note about the kitchen.
Keep the teacups Peteris painted
on a safe shelf:
one is for love,
one is for faith's long–enduring self.

Author's Note: My fiancé and I hoped to live in Latvia in a farmhouse he owned. "Good fishing among birches and pines!" was the claim printed on a postcard I had received from him.

Elisavietta Ritchie

IN KRALJEVO

October flows in rivers boiling chill.
A Balkan storm combs off all gilded leaves.
Gray sheep are strewn across a rumpled hill.
Strung peppers redden underneath the eaves.
Five piglets probe the purpled cabbage rows.
A fiddler charms his goat around the field.
The bees fly heavily. Gold honey glows
In jars along our sill. Jam pots are sealed.
Ten pumpkins heap beside the wooden gate.
Our harvest in this land of marigolds:
Although we meet and love each other late,
In Gyspy summer smoke of burning souls
Twirls high, entangles in a scarlet vine.
We press our grapes, drink all the garnet wine.

Author's Note: In 1979 I was a US sponsored visiting poet throughout a peaceful former Yugoslavia. From a writers' conference in Belgrade we traveled around Serbia. Kraljevo seemed a still life with the country's past and future suspended.

Jody Bolz

WAYANG

On the train across Java
we slept in a knot:
my head in your lap,
your head on my back,

two hundred miles
through the tropical dark
in shuddering third-class.
At every major stop,

a skirmish of shouted light—
vendors hawking tea and rice
to sleep-drugged passengers—
receded in a rush,

the jasmine-scented silence
sweet and abrupt.
When the station's speakers
keened their exit song,

the train lurched on.
Whirr of palm and banyan,
gibbous moon, skewed night sky—
green stars above the village mosque

jumped and scuttled by
in deranged constellations.
We stretched, switched positions:
your hair red as rosestalks

against my faded dress,
my braids strict shadows
on your moonlit back,
our fractured dreams resettling....

Knowing Stones

Outside Bandung at dawn,
I shook my buzzing limbs,
cracked our dirty window open
to mountain air.

A boy wrapped in a shawl
shot past in the brightening field.
One child, then another—
a horde of barefoot children

in tattered pastel sweaters
raced beside the tracks,
calling out for coins,
for candies,

falling far behind us
by the time we reached
their shanties: tin roofs
at the rail–bed's edge—

doorways set in sloping walls,
a threshing floor,
an open sewer.
As our train slowed

a pregnant girl,
waist–long hair undone,
stepped out of a hovel
fastening her sarong.

We passed her without speaking,
tugging at the taut string
of our marriage
as it rose over rice–fields,

climbing into monsoon clouds,
swaying there—spiraling—
not some *thing*,
not a child's kite:

our common life, flown
above another Asian city
in the year we made a home
out of our bodies.

Author's Note: Twenty years ago, the "bus–train" from Bali to West Java carried travellers through the night from the palm–covered tropics into the highlands near Bandung, a popular hill station during Dutch colonial days. At each train station en route, the departure signal was a plaintive rendition of a koto song—"Cherry Blossoms"—an eerie reminder of Japan's brief dominance over Indonesia during WWII

The Land Keeps Unholy Secrets

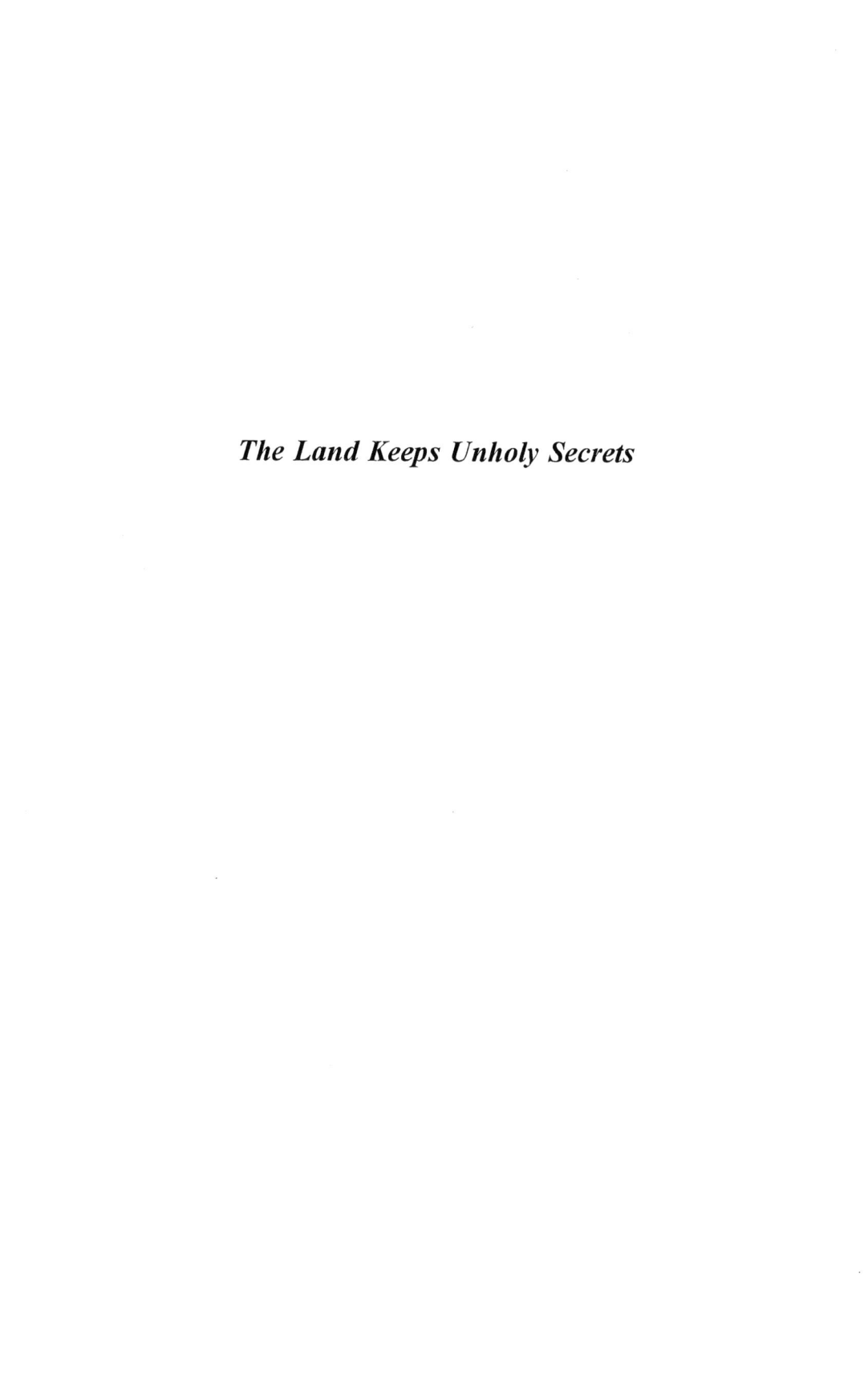

Poet-travelers, seeking the unforseen, seldom leave home without their sharpened tools of observation and compassion. Hence they often find themselves in places where injustice is waiting to be named and have its story told. Not necessarily political by nature, such travelers may discover that it is not possible to be in a place without experiencing a history of oppression that lingers, almost palpably, in the air. Atrocities and colossal wrongs endured by our fellow mortals have somehow imprinted themselves into the landscape.

Although its locations may be shifting, a common inhumanity still plays itself out around the world. Whether the perpetrators of injustice have been colonists, oppressive regimes, or merely the complacent establishment of a given place and time, we would do well to recognize elements of ourselves in them as we contemplate the devastation they have left in these places.

Anna Citrino

SHEEP

"This world is not my home, I'm just passing through.
My treasures are laid up somewhere beyond the blue.
The angels beckon me from heaven's open door
And I can't feel at home in this world anymore."
                              —traditional.

Dark men scatter on the long stretch of beach.
The thin membrane of turquoise water
blends into the far sky.
Underneath the sand
wafer-shaped plastic mines wait,
left from the war.

Clear the beach.
That's what the man said.
Make the country safe.
The sheep have already gone before.
Got to finish the leftovers.

The small, dark man places his foot
forward on the shining sand watching his shadow stretch,
hoping the grains where he steps have not shifted,
hoping he can get the money
to feed his family back in Bangladesh
where the sacred Ganges flows—
Mother of all life songs
and death dances.

He dances for her barefoot,
weaving his dark body
between the others,
making a river

across the fiery silica, a faith walker,
praying silently for the moon
and her soft white light to bless him
with coolness when the heat of
his maimed limb
stops burning.

Author's Note: After the Persian Gulf War, Kuwait's beaches needed to be cleared of land mines. First sheep were sent across the beaches, but this was not totally effective. Officials offered to pay Bangladeshies money if they would walk the beaches. They risked becoming maimed, but many, in their poverty, accepted the risk in order to gain money for their families.

Tom McCarthy

PROSTHESIS FACTORY IN PHNOM PENH

for Leah Melnick

A wooden block shaped just so
a hole carved into the top
padded with rags
strapped to the blunt end
of an amputated leg
with leather belts cut from
an army field pack
so the guy can stump
downtown and get a job.

Pair of bicycle wheels slung together
one small wooden wheel in front
sticks and ropes with a
bit of plank for the seat
for narrow useless hips
skinny legs bound with rags
at the knees and ankles
so he can wheel home to the village
to plow muddy rice fields
behind the great gray water buffalo.

A sharp knife strapped
to a handless wrist
the guy with one arm
whittled a leg for
the guy with no legs.

The factory foreman's face was
half stitched leather, half scar tissue
one red eye gazed out
from a lidless socket
more a hole in his skull
as he carefully measured
with a string
all four stumps of a former soldier.
Held by a strap, a leather flap
covered the foreman's mouth.
He worked silently.

In the tree–leafy courtyard
of this former temple
water–stained walls
moldy thatch roof
sat several dozen people
on benches, on palm stumps
with squalling babies
cradled in what arms they had
among busted statuary, tangled vines
sleeping there at night, too
camped out on straw mats
dozens of them, ex–soldiers,
wounded farmers, shattered schoolchildren
waiting expectantly and patiently
waiting and waiting
to walk home
hold a child's hand.

Author's Note: The former temple Wat Than was converted to a prosthesis factory by an international charitable organization in order to provide jobs and artificial limbs for the many victims of land mines in Cambodia. Leah Melnick was a colleague and friend; she was killed in a helicopter crash in Bosnia in 1998.

Willa Schneberg

THE HOTEL CAMBODIANA

It's always tea time at the Cambodiana.
We don't care about history here.
We own the manor.
We are the British in India,
the Italians in Eritrea,
the Dutch in Indonesia.
As far as we're concerned *Cambodge*
will always be a French baguette.

If Cambodia were designed by Disney
it would be the Cambodiana
with orange tiled pitched roofs and facades
turned up at the ends like leprechaun shoes,
where Khmer culture is an *apsara* with Barbie's body,
and stone *Avalokitesvaras'* full–lipped mouths
smiling beatifically adorn whiskey glasses.

We are too busy toasting ourselves
to hear the bulldozers flattening the huts
of the squatters outside the gate,
who come at the demolitionists with axes,
stupidly refusing to give up their land, and
accept who they are:
never a well–stocked wine cellar,
always an olive in the bottom of the martini glass.

Author's Note: In 1992/93 I worked in Phnom Penh, Cambodia for the UN Transitional Authority. The Cambodiana on the banks of the Tonle Sap was the most elegant hotel in town, the accommodations of choice for affluent businessmen and diplomats.

Apsara: Khmer for heavenly dancer.
Avalokitesvaras: Over 200 faces adorn Bayon's towers. They represent the face of god–king Jayavarman VII.

Christopher Conlon

SOWETO

You can take a tour bus. It's pink. Right from the Carlton five-star, downtown Johannesburg, through the suburbs, past an extensive coloured neighborhood, eighteen kilometers: and on the way the well-dressed black guide tells you through a faulty microphone about the thirty-five townships, the one million official inhabitants, the two million unofficial ones, and the thousand deaths that occur monthly: most of "not natural causes." At first it seems not so bad. Crowding, yes, poverty; but houses, at least, real brick houses like little jails, electricity, supermarkets, patches of grass. Mandela's old house, his wife's new mansion, the first beer garden to be burned out in '76—still a black husk. Tutu's church, and his house, on the wall of which is spray-painted: GO HOME YOU WHITE RACIST TOURIST PIGS AND TAKE YOUR BLACK STOOGE TOUR GUIDE WITH YOU.

You snap photos.

A stop at an orphanage, where blanketed infants are lined up—twenty or more—in cardboard boxes on the floor. The toddlers, having not yet caught on, cavort for the strangers and their cameras. But soon there are no more brick houses, no more cute clean babies, no more grass. Soon there is only a vista of corrugated tin shacks: dilapidated, packed together like a mass grave, sinking like old men into the earth. One tap for three hundred people. Stench and brown smoke: dirty men, sagging women standing before their homes, staring blankly at the people gazing through their bus windows as through television screens at an unreal city in a distant country, staring blankly at the pink people who are but a few feet from them in their air-conditioned pink bus, soon to be heading back to their air-conditioned pink hotels, snapping cameras with their fat pink fingers—

I was there, Uncle Bob will say, *O those poor people!;* but a few feet away, yes, but no, not really so close, still worlds away, safely hidden behind pink plexiglass: still back in London, Montreal, Boston, Johannesburg: a thousand worlds distant in unreal cities of their own.

Knowing Stones

This is Soweto, the guide says as the bus begins to move again, as the children, having not yet caught on, laugh and wave and chase after it; and you stare after them, frozen, petrified, trying not to hear the cluckings of sympathy as the cameras snap and snap like whips, like slaps, and you think, try to think, only of clean, clear water splashing onto your face: dissolving the skin: the color running like make-up into the soil, soaking away, fading: and leaving behind only that which is pure, colorless, untainted. New.

Author's Note: This poem was written in 1989, just before South Africa began its historic changeover to majority rule. But sadly, while some things have changed—the phrase "coloured," referring to people of mixed-race heritage, is passing from fashion—the lives of most people in Soweto are still much as I described them here.

Leza Lowitz

AT THE SENBITSUKA

The subject was war that day in the newspaper
(and what subject found there isn't?)
when they discovered the tomb of a thousand noses
covered by weeds, overgrown with grasses past.

No apology was forthcoming
four hundred years later
when all the smells of summer
drifted up from the archaeologist's shovel.

Hardly heroic now, these noses
of generals and shoemakers,
merchants and poor farmer's sons,
each like an ancient stone lantern

whose light has too long been blown out
against a dark history
buried deep in the peaceful red clay
of an old potter's town.

Author's Note: The Senbitsuka (1,000–Nose Tomb) was discovered near Bizen, in Okayama prefecture, Japan, on September 24, 1992. 20,000 Koreans were killed in 1592 by Japanese forces who amputated their noses, bringing them back to Japan as war spoils. The noses were taken back to South Korea's Cholla Province in 1992.

Deborah Byrne

SHADOW POEM

Birds ignite in midair. Plants shield reverse silhouettes.
A man leaves the memorial of his outline on the steps of a bank.
 —August 6, 1945, 8:16 AM Hiroshima time. Little Boy explodes.
"Just as I looked up at the sky, there was a flash of white light
and the green in the plants looked in that light like the color of dry leaves."
 —A woman remembers when she was five years old.
My uncle is being chased through streets at the hypocenter.
There is no one there, he knows he can never escape.
 —Dream, 1974.

I. Psalm

Concrete walls display shadows
that have lost their people.
They ignite memory,
swoon in flickering daylight,
still themselves in collective knowing.

II. Lamentation

No writer will save us with poetics.
We look for uncertain passage to lost worlds. The sun
is cold against our embedded prints near twisted swingsets
and fishmarkets we once worked. Oh, how cruel the Buddha
who resides here.

III. Ezekiel

Shadow cannot flee the empty streets,
from time and space man did not know
he could dream. A monstrous crane flies
in the direction of Nagasaki—
shadow added to this procession.

Author's Note: My uncle Walt Hazelbaker, who had been a military photographer on the atomic bomb project, sometimes told me his feelings about what he had been involved with. In later life he did pro bono photography of burn victims for lawsuits on their behalf.

It is said that those who survived the bombing of Hiroshima did not acknowledge the existence of those images burnt into concrete which I saw there three years ago.

Claire T. Feild

THE TARO FIELDS

The taro plants flush green,
Early rising, fluent within their rectangular
Flats, yet lying in state before Ruler Row,
Cliffs that bond together,
Preventing the plants from borrowing
Foreign breaths from the mountain's
Other side,
The mysterious side that cannot
Care when the plants will be
Sullenly harvested by tight brown
Skins that arch their backs just like
The one-lane bridge that provides
An outlet for both a legitimate harvest
And the men's itinerant emotions.

Author's Note: Fields of taro, which is used for making poi, can be seen from the Hanalei Valley Overlook in Princeville, Kauai. As I watched these fields being worked by Polynesian men, I was transported to my childhood in the Mississippi Delta of the 1950s and the sight of African Americans bent over the cotton.

Andrew Epstein

CARIB'S LEAP

In Sauters, up a long steep hill,
past hundreds of clamoring kids
in white uniforms, black arms swinging
against the glare of sun on white fabric,
they sing, we don't understand, and one throws
nuts in the open window
strikes my open eyes
and the guide assures me
kids are kids wherever you go
and winding through angular streets
to a plaque on a fence on the edge
of a hilltop graveyard, fresh flowers
stirring next to makeshift markers,
corridor through the names of the local dead,
lined by tall grasses and touched by moist wind,
a plaque to mark this spot –
the finish line to a famous race
where Europe's choking sickness caught
the other half of the world by surprise,
warriors turned lemming, every single
Carib stepped off this edge of the green world
and plummeted into a dingy weed-covered plaque.

Carib now, Carib remains, Carib
etched in yellow blue
label of that beer broad–shouldered men
with sharp cheekbones
drink along the side of every curve of road.
In the distance the Grenadines jut,
the hunched shoulders of friends
not too near the victim at an accident scene.
They stay there like a tease for those who jumped,
like an unpronounceable
word that could save a life if uttered.
There's no picture to take,
just space where the land ends, and
the cliff takes away the certainties
of the long–grassed graveyard of the freshly dead.

Endless sun still beats on the cemetery,
kids scream and circle us, with their slingshots
aim stones at gulls
that hover near the cliff,
shooting volleys into the air over the sea,
trying to smack the breathing out of
anything their rocks can reach.

Author's Note: Like many Caribbean islands, Grenada had a long history of European colonization, rebellion, and unrest. Soon after French colonists took over the island in 1650, the indigenous Caribs fought back against their invaders. Armed with only bows and arrows, the Caribs were no match for the Europeans' guns. Driven to the northern end of the island, they chose to throw themselves off a cliff into the sea rather than be captured or killed. Carib is also the name of a popular beer in Grenada. The Grenadines are a group of small islands to the north.

Carol Kanter

SCAPEGOATS

White hulks of cattle claim one pasture site;
brown species stay apart in their own field;
and cows seamed of amoeboid black and white
segregate on acres fenced and sealed.
But where four corners touch, three meet to deal—
one white, one brown, one black and white—they stand
head to head to head, a solemn wheel
of switching tails. Each airs his herd's demands...

And while those three chew over pacts, on lands
nearby ewes stroll, necks bent to reap wet grass—
the gentle hills a–litter with their lambs.
They're unaware that present bliss could pass;
that whatever promises steer pledge to keep,
their summit talk cannot bode well for sheep.

Author's Note: Near Waitangi, New Zealand. In the 1840 Treaty of Waitangi, Great Britain granted military protection to chiefs from some Maori tribes in exchange for lands (essentially New Zealand's North Island.) Since native cultures had no concept of land ownership, heated debate continues in New Zealand over the legality of this treaty.

Elisavietta Ritchie

STEALING BLACKBERRIES AT PORT ARTHUR

Boys got flogged for less,
jailed, deported to this
chilly British gulag.

Such huge berries—
I would risk
everything for them.

Nostalgic colonists
transported roots
from distant gardens.

Now vines lace up the gully
strewn with rubble. Thorns
scratch, tendrils wrap

crumbling sandstone blocks
tumbled from the burned
church and broken jail

convicts built before
they died of hunger, cold
or punishment.

Today three white mares,
ten brown steers,
a flock of farmyard geese

and a pair of dark ducks
graze this paddock,
observe my theft.

Ancient bones and blood
fed these onyx berries. My stains
betray their succulence.

Yet this pilfered feast
commemorates
bitter histories...

Could even one despairing man
steal away from forest or quarry
to snatch a handful of berries

before the birds?
Or a mate, assigned the task,
dumped him in a pit

in common anonymity
to nurture rhododendrons,
eucalyptus, berries fat as these.

Author's Note: Port Arthur, Tasmania was the harshest of the penal colonies to which the British sent their convicts, here especially the recidivists and "trouble makers." Port Arthur still looks like a university village with stone buildings (all built by convicts, often wearing leg irons) amid green lawns. Escape either by land or sea was almost impossible, and thousands of convicts died here. Visitors claim to have seen a number of their ghosts.

Sandra Olson

OF BARRACKS AND BEE STINGS

There's no more terror
at Perm 36,
only mosquitoes, bees, horseflies
rising in waves.
A prison with its doors flung wide,
encircled by its own rubble.

Somehow evil cannot last,
eventually corroding,
collapsing on itself,
like the tsar, the chief, the torturer
with their rashes, ulcers, cancers.

Hatred, fear, jealousy linger,
pollinated by the buzzing hordes,
who circle, dart, and dive for the face,
with a suicidal instinct to injure.

It was never really possible
to leave this place
unscarred.
Half–hidden shards of glass,
barbed wire, rusty nails.
Clouds darken,
the wind turns cold,
the return
of every starved and beaten ghost,
swirling with memories,
flashes of pain,
visions growing clearer
with one eye swollen shut.

Author's Note: The Perm Region is 700 miles east of Moscow, at the edge of the Ural Mountains. Its pastoral landscape of farms and birch forests hid some of the Soviet regime's most infamous gulags. Many prominent dissidents were imprisoned there. In 1995 I was among the volunteers from Russia, Europe, and the US who came together to restore the main barracks at Perm 36. It has been dedicated as a museum and memorial.

Kelly Cherry

REPORT FROM AN UNNAMED CITY

In the square in the center of our city, there flows
unstoppingly a fountain of despair
from which we drink, hoping in this simple way to
acquire immunity to hope, for
hope is the knife that separates us from ourselves.

At night, we gather in small groups
in small, locked houses. Rain ticks against the windowpanes.
A fugitive moon slips from cloud to cloud,
seeking cover. We are still alive,
thank God. Our neighbors have been less lucky—

wiped out, like an insect colony.

Author's Note: This unnamed city happened to have been in the Soviet Union. Today it could be located in many countries of the world.

Kelly Cherry

LIVADIYA PALACE, SITE OF THE YALTA CONFERENCE

Here and here and here,
They sat and signed.
You take that country, why don't you.
We'll keep this one, if you don't mind.

And nobody minded.

The Black Sea was blue.
Salt air burned in the bright sun
Like sea salt in a Georgian stew.

And flags flew.

Sick, old, mad,
They sat and signed.

Who knew,
Who, then, knew...

The flags flew.
Dinner was fine,
Followed by brandy
And port wine.

Author's Note: While the Soviet Union was still in place, I visited Livadiya Palace in Yalta, where the Yalta agreements were signed by Roosevelt, Churchill, and Stalin in 1945.

Walter Bargen

RUSSIAN PARLIAMENT 8/20/91

In a glassy rain the crowd stands alone.
Ten thousand umbrellas weep along their
gaunt ribs. Street lamps streak and puddle

in the cracks between cobbles. Pried out
and hefted in hands, they are elementary
lessons in the history of resistance.

The daily life of cars and buses comes to a stop.
Tanks direct traffic. Death's wet mile
smiles from both sides of the barricades.

The long night is coming and they will wait.
Others say it has arrived and no one needs
to wait. Already a few names have lost

their bodies and float above the crowd.
Long ropes of grief are pulled from throats
and heroes wait for their monuments, as always.

Author's Note: On August 19th, 1991, Soviet hardline politicians, backed by security forces, attempted to overthrow the newly emerging Russian government. On August 20th as many as 150,000 citizens in support of the new government surrounded the parliament building, throwing up barricades and defying Soviet soldiers and tanks. Speaking to the Soviet forces, Boris Yeltsin said, "You can erect a throne of bayonets, but you cannot sit on it for long." On August 21st the coup attempt failed.

Michele Battiste

PRAGUE'S REVENGE

You are not generous—you Prague, you Praha
boasting scratched and sketched lines that draw down the clouds,
the floor of your negligent heaven, damp and full of colic

Your scars are much stronger
earthbound and everywhere they crisscross all bridges and roads,
the seams holding you still

How can you be so greedy?
hoarding and hiding what is and used to be alive
I do not want your high-priced crystal, your tradition of garnet
glittering pieces of take home tourism
permitting a few hundred thousand lies claiming intimacy
I am not your John

I want to crawl beneath your cobblestones
like you've crawled beneath my skin,
making me bend and beat my heels
against your precious steepled views

Such a slow process, this breaking into the inside,
this burrowing down
but your history has grown so thick it will not yield
and protects fiercely your pulses
You could be hurt again. Unintentionally, but still you could be.

So you demand me naked and cold and thinned
and you promise me that I will not be afraid
Then you send me home with fingertips cut open
and bruised from the long digging
that never surfaced

And you have one more scar to call your own

Author's Note: Prague, capital of the Czech Republic, has survived centuries of oppression and war. In 1989 the streets of Prague's Nove Mesto (New Town) gave birth to the Velvet Revolution, an uprising that liberated the country from 41 years of Communist rule. Today the "city of dreams" struggles to make peace with its legacy of oppression and to forge a future that will reconcile autonomy with its celebrated but martyred role as the heart of Europe.

Elisavietta Ritchie
SARAJEVO

I. June 1914

The Archduke is being driven
from maneuvers
to the gala lunch.

The shuttle shoots
to the selvage
on hundreds of looms.

A watchman dreams of figs.

The plausible trajectory
has not yet met its mark.

Skinny ghosts spin
from the strings
of the village fiddler.

A cadet at attention too long
sways in the sun.

A shopkeeper counts
his coffee beans.
Flies land in bowls
of honeyed milk.

Heat and dust and blood
rise from the quays
in a furl of mosquitoes.

II. October 1979

Rain slides down
entire horizons
of onion domes,
washes spires
in darkening tears.

Cold slips inside
thin coats,
soaked shoes.

Unquiet mud oozes
over bald cobblestones,
hides shadows
of old footprints.

In the riverbank park
snowberries glow
death white.

Parapets are decked
with maroon petunias,
velvety but

the bridge is too
narrow to bear
all that history.

Magpies stalk
the wasted river
for minnows, flies,
their own
warped reflections.

Downriver the waters
run red: perhaps effluent
from a textile mill.

Prayer unwinds from a minaret.
Tombstones crowd
within cracked walls
and rusted grilles.

In a shuttered apartment
a battered trumpet
and accordion
attempt a minuet.
On these windy quays
I also wait
at a crossroad.

Had Gavrilo Princep arrived
in this colder season
his fingers might
have shivered too much
on the trigger.

But there are always
other assassins...

Author's Note: In 1979, a visiting poet in Yugoslavia, I had time to wander around Sarajevo and stan
in the footprints of the Archduke's assassin. It seemed a dark, brooding city, especially in the cold rai
of October. During recent civil conflicts I was asked to write a new section, but what was happening t
Sarajevo was so terrible that no poem I could write would describe or honor the horror.

Steve Barfield

LORCA AT THE WALL

"And let my blood on the field
Make sweet and rosy mud
Where weary peasants
Sink their hoes,"
 —Federico Garcia Lorca, "Cicada", August 3, 1918, *Book of Poems*.

Yes even Lorca at the wall in fascist Spain.
During the darkest midnight of the spirit
they took this lyric poet of light
out into an evening of splintering crystal.
A single lamp post stands against the shadows.

Lorca was not known by the fascists
though they knew the change he represented,
the same change time expects of us all.

Near the ancient olive groves of Granada
with a booted spur at the rim of the fountain
dip the color from the old moon
and touch the mysteries of the Arab.
There was a gentle liquid sound
in the water garden
of this most Moorish castle Alhambra.

A black cape from a prior century
that was quietly folded in upon itself.

Consult with the prophet Cassandra at another wall.
Turn to the people with the terror of that truth
that their children will be different than themselves.
God save us from the righteous,
for they are without mercy.

The wall is a bougainvillea and stone delineation
that wanders through the fertile soil of Andalusia.
A wall that will not contain:
his truth
his life of poetry.

His shadow is surprised by the sudden light
and slowly releases its silhouette.

Author's Note: In August, 1936 the facist Falangists took the poet Federico Garcia Lorca, along with a few other luckless souls, out on a lonely road rising up from the Spanish village Alfacar. On a moonless night near an olive grove, all were summarily shot and buried in an unmarked grave.

Alan Elyshevitz

POLAND, 1990

Krakow slumbers, Bytom glows.
In between lies quiescent land,
soft and hushed
like the cloakroom of a synagogue.

Listen for the flat faint voice
of the camp survivor who chanted
kaddish at the lip of a burial pit,
or the one who spoke of vermin stench
impounded in the walls,
or the inmate intellectual
who interpreted dreams of warm shoes.

The tales have all been told,
scraped from aged vocal chords
like cinnamon from the laurel tree
or scrawled in arthritic calligraphy.

And still this earth responds
to dung with greenery.
A beast of burden drags a plough
through superstitious fields,
but shuns the fallow ground
around the camp museum.

Author's Note: In southern Poland, the remains of the Nazi concentration camp at Auschwitz–Birkenau is now a museum operated by the Polish government.

Leza Lowitz

BERLIN WALL

What is a wall
but a particular kind of dream

of a promised land
never arrived at,

some few coins in your pocket
you could be jailed for,

a range of impossible
choices.

What is a wall but a wooden bridge
swaying under awkward feet

all those horns honking unseen
and the disappointment of waiting

on a reception line that
never ends and never begins.

What is a dream but
boxes of sponges and books

photos of families in clipped
winter dances

burning into memory like
the last few stones of gypsy coal.

What is a wall but a
wind that blows empty

and a scarecrow, a scarecrow
repelling what ripens.

Author's Note: Written four years before the Berlin Wall came down, this poem was read at a public gathering just after the San Francisco earthquake of October 17, 1989. Everything is fragile, everything crumbles in its own time, but some walls should come down by sheer force of human will.

Cassie Premo Steele

DOS MARIAS

It was in a quiet white
underground room
of the *Museo Nacional*
on my last day
in Ecuador that I saw her:
the pregnant virgin,
Maria Embarazada,
her chin slightly chipped,
but belly softly rounded
off in wood, made plain
by many bruises.
The only other was in Spain,
a sign said.

I could get to her
if I followed a red
string straight across the middle
of the world to another
who waits, and wonders
what happened to her sisters,
every other Mary
who was *embarazada*
and then *destruida. Destruida,*
a sign read.
Only *dos Marias* remain,
separated by two worlds
like the double meanings
of all the words in the same
body: *embarazada, pleine,
schuld,* float, sink, long,
the list goes on and on.

Author's Note: National Museum in Quito, Ecuador. *Embarazada,* Spanish for pregnant, connotes the English *embarrassed. Pleine* is French for pregnant and full; *schuld* is German for both guilt and debt.

Margaret Blaker

UNDERWORLD PALACE SCENE WITH BEHEADING

The palace girls are lovely, slender heads
molded to cylinders like Maya vases,
hair trimmed to next–to–nothing to set off
the slant of brows, the little glyphic ears.

Beneath his screech–owl feather crown, their lord
from his low dais smiles a toothless smile,
fastens one little beauty's bracelet,
his jaded hand upon her jade–lit wrist.

The girls pour chocolate, but one has seen–
behind their backs—the captive, naked, bound.
(He's not a lord: his head is much too round.)
The executioners, in grinning masks,

direct stone axes to their artful task.
A rabbit scribe, in journalistic zeal,
bends to his folded, jaguar–pelt–bound tome,
takes it all down in flowing monochrome.

This is Xibalba, but it's just like home,
the mundane Maya world...or even ours,
where every day some captives lose their heads–
outsiders, naturally, not from the local realm.

But with their blood the local gods are fed.

Author's Note: This scene appears on a Classic Maya vase in the Princeton Art Museum. It is in "Codex style," which refers to the flowing curvilinear black or brown line used in certain Maya vases.

Darrell g.h. Schramm

BETWEEN CARTAGENA AND BARANQUILLA

I never knew what they were looking for.
The other times were also like the first:
At the border of not a country but
a province, the old bus, yellow and blue,
metal and wood, would rattle to a stop.
Four, five men in khaki, guns like infants
in their arms, would stare with careful faces
at us as one would board, interrogate
two passengers or three, then order all
outside. Machine gun motions formed us left
and right lines. A *gringo,* I was never
searched or questioned. The lush, tropical air
hung humid with silence and fear. Once on
our way, someone was always left behind.

Author's Note: In Colombia, a beautiful but violent country, kidnapping, torture, killing, and other gross human rights violations by police, paramilitary groups, armed forces, and guerrilla bands, motivated by cocaine, emeralds, political power, and/or revenge, continue to take place.

Jonathan Harrington

SMILE

This morning
in some small republic below the equator
a man brushes his teeth.
The stench of a million corpses is on his breath.
His blue eyes are the color of a frozen hand
and his lips are purplish and swollen with blood
as if, like a vulture, he has fed on carrion.
He is brushing his smile for the foreign press corps.
It is a genuine smile,
for he smiles easily and often.
He has smiled through a thousand executions.
He has pulled the trigger while smiling.
He's really a wonderful man.
It is not easy being a dictator.
It involves getting quite a bit of blood on one's pants
and sometimes white Panama hat.
And the stench of corpses lingers on one's breath,
like the general's, who brushes his teeth constantly.
He carries his toothbrush with him at all times
even to meetings with CIA agents to plot murders.
After the meetings, the general brushes his teeth.
He is very concerned about cleanliness
and looking and eating right.

Author's Note: Somewhere in South America.

Carolyne Wright

THE ROOM

for Margaret Gibson, R.N.

She stood in the room where Allende died.
It was two months later,
Armistice Day, 1973,
and she was on a package tour
for which all refunds had been cancelled.
Below the bombed-out windows
with their twisted grillework,
Pinochet's troops patrolled the streets,
and she wore a scarlet poppy
for that other war—Flanders Field
and the black-edged telegram
that had stopped her father's face
in its frame on the mantelpiece.

For years she would not tell this story:
how she walked through Santiago's
rubble-strewn streets until soldiers
leaped from a van with naked bayonets
and surrounded her, ripping her camera
from her shoulder. All afternoon in the *cuartel*
she showed them blurry Polaroids
of palm trees and big hotels,
and told them she knew nothing.
She wasn't working for anyone.
As late sun slanted through the one window's
iron bars, the *comandante* suddenly
relented. "We have something special
to show you." His tone said
You'd better not refuse.

A guard led her through cratered beds
and shattered statuary of the garden,
into the high-ceilinged room
already beginning to fill with twilight.

Knowing Stones

Everything was as they had left it.
She gazed a long time
at the red plush chair,
the heavy desk with bullet marks,
scorched books piled knee deep
on the floor.
              "Communist books,"
the guard said, shifting
the rifle to his shoulder.
There was a battered telephone
on the desktop, and a letter
handwritten in Spanish,
the fountain pen lying across it
where the words trailed off.

She knew no Spanish.
The guard stepped to the window.
She wanted to take the letter
or engrave it in her thoughts
for her friends outside, but the guard
turned back and there was no way
she could go beyond this warning.
She studied the prescription bottle
by the inkwell: nitroglycerin
he took for his congested heart.
On the floor under the sideboard
a whiskey bottle on its side, cracked open,
spill of dark residue beside it.
"*El Presidente* liked his booze,"
the guard smirked, as if
that justified everything.

Her eyes had been saving the blood
for last. In the failing light
the dark stains stood out black—
his last call to his wife,
his farewell to Chile on the radio
when he knew they were coming for him.

Spatter on the walls still echoing
the burst door, the rifle barrels
raised, automatic fire going on and on.
Vanishing in shadow the pool
of himself into which he fell.

Outside, wail of the curfew sirens,
footsteps of those who could be shot
on sight for delaying. "Don't worry,
we escort you back," the guard said.
"We know how to treat our friends."

For years she would feel the click
of the safety catch, chill of steel
at her temple, the poppy's crimson
deepening on her breast.
She said *No thank you*
and walked out.
If soldiers tried to stop her
she would turn and face them
as she still wanted to believe
he had.

Author's Note: For several days after the September 11, 1973 coup in which the elected government of Salvador Allende was overthrown, spokesmen for the new regime claimed that the dead President had committed suicide in his office during the aerial bombardment of the Moneda, the presidential palace. The suicide weapon was alleged to have been a submachine gun presented to Allende by Fidel Castro.

M. Eliza Hamilton Abegunde

KEEPING WATCH: ON ROUTE TO BRAZIL

for Captain Bill Pinkney

He tells me about the harness that shackles him to the vessel, its high quality nylon designed to keep him safe. How the sound like heavy metal against thunder recalls the lost memory of the collar that choked him every time he breathed.

I want to tell him that the teak beneath my feet lives even after cutting. How it carries the root stories of oak and pecan, ebony and baobab. For every naked inch of my flesh that touches a plank, I mark my location with grave sites not longitude.

I have known this since birth: I am the last one left because centuries ago, the ship which carried 425 of us arrived carrying only me. On nights I dare put one sole on deck, my own voice frightens me as I sing the stories of people whose tongues have been cut, but who insist on speaking.

He tells me the voices of children wake him at night. Their laughter surrounds him. Their tiny fingers pat him on the shoulder and rub his balding head. Then he lets the waves carry them where he cannot follow and where I have already gone.

They bang themselves against the hull of my bunk until I am bruised by their urging that I am the vessel being carried. I want to tell him about the screaming inside my head since Barbados. Sister, they say, I have left my story here: under your arm pit, in your left eye. In your womb. Remember: Memory is your gift to us. Remember the chains that bind us, make us whole.

He tells me softly: You've not had the benefit of night watch when the Ancestors walk above deck. I laugh quietly and want to tell him: It is not only above deck that we walk. But I am silent. One day, we will speak of the things that haunt us.

Author's Note: I traveled with Captain William Pinkney on the S.S. Sortilege to retrace part of the Middle Passage routes used to bring Africans to North and South America and the Caribbean.

Oh, the People You'll Meet

Stones, harder even than the bony skeleton, are the last visible remains of once vibrant life in ancient urban centers. So we go to visit the ruins. But in distant regions we also meet the people for whom the place is now home. And while the stones imprint themselves on our memories, the fragile or robust lives we encounter around them move us even more deeply.

In exotic places we see both the magically real and the painfully real. In some ways the people we meet there may remind us of ourselves; in others, they challenge our values. The simple beauty of their lives inspires us to honor the everyday.

Let these poets introduce you to some memorable people so that you may join their festivities and mourn their suffering.

Thea Sullivan

ON THE CHAO PHRAYA, BANGKOK

That morning we balanced on the rocking pier,
squinted into the haze. The sun had cut itself
into a thousand shards, highrise windows
flashing a silvery glare.
Fan-tail boats trailed garlands,
blossoms skimming the bronze
river, and boat hands whistled, slicing
the din. But what I remember

is not this, not the spicy–sweet smell of garbage
leeching, or the temple, Wat Arun,
we were waiting to see, its carved spires cloaked
in scaffolds of bamboo, warning us away.
Instead, I see the man with a thatch of white hair,
t-shirt stretched across his ribs, who padded
barefoot toward us, bearing a flimsy plate.
How he stopped and squatted at the edge
of the dock, veins in his calves rising.
How he lay the plate down, pressed
fingertips together, lowered his head in prayer.

After a time, he straightened and turned
up the wooden ramp to the cool
inside the shack, his solemn wife, the dogs sleeping.
Water sloshing through slats at their feet.
His offering to the river:
a donut, frosted in pink,
and anchored in it, a stick of incense
sending up its fragile thread.

Author's Note: The Chao Phraya River is in many ways the heart of Bangkok, Thailand, a city once called "the Venice of the East." The wide, metallic–looking river is a main artery of transportation, a hub of commerce in the form of floating markets, a rare source of solace in a noisy city, even, as I glimpsed on this morning, an object of worship and devotion.

Michael Waters

"NIGHT IN THE TROPICS" (1858-59?)

"Lack of listeners did not deter Louis Moreau Gottschalk, living on the edge of a Guadeloupe volcano in 1859, from giving piano recitals to the universe."
—Edmund Morris, *The Romance of the Piano.*

Assuming *rain,* the exotic
species flare up like gas-flames
released from the earth, then settle on hibiscus
branches as the arpeggios shower down.
But the blossoms remain dry, their wings
dry, and only the spattering
notes keep them pinned to their trees, leaves
and insects blending in infinite
varieties.
      And the birds who pluck rare
butterflies from air, not finding them there,
assume *nightfall,* so return to their nests,
tongues stiff, though the sun slips
its staff of light through the canopies,
                        & so on
upward through the great chain of being, all
the bird–eating snakes, the snake–eating
birds, till the selection seems to halt,
Louis Moreau Gottschalk
slightly unnerved as he swabs the moisture
from the strings, shuts the lid of the Chickering,
then steps from the terrace into his room
to allow the universe to resume.

Author's Note: Morris's essay appeared in *The New Yorker.* One sentence, used here as an epigraph, triggered the poem.

Richard Beban

OUR LADY OF THE PIGEONS

At the Piazza San Marco a woman stands,
arms horizontal, waiting
to take flight. Her hands are full of stale bread,
her body is suet. She can barely be seen
for the pigeons that cover her,
croon throaty promises,
rustle wings like wedding silk.
In her feather cocoon she wishes
her eyes were millet, offers them,
eager beaks peck,
swallow the gelatin of sight. Red feet clutch,
claws hold tight & all take flight at once
she ascends in a flurry of beating wings
the cathedral below her, jealous, landlocked stone.

Author's Note: In Venice, Italy I saw a woman in the Piazza completely covered by pigeons.

Bill Yake

WOMAN KNITTING OVER FLORENCE

The summer is old, comfortable and thirsty
half a millennium after the Rebirth.
It has not rained for months.
I sleep in a cool, stone room until noon,

then starting at the Ponte Vecchio, span
the still, small Arno; wind up pathways—step
by worn stone step to lawns, fortified and
stretched out above a thousand red tile roofs.

Here a woman is knitting straw afternoons
together—for lovers and card players. She sits
among narrow trees of sharp green shadows,
works steadily between voices in the rare shade

of dominos. Below, the Arno dries hourly as if
it were painted this morning. Overlooking the river
I have walked beside music, a cappella chatter,
and this woman knitting afternoon to afternoon.

Her needles click and flash; and although
the sun is always rising and always setting,
it stops and hangs a measure in the sky transfixed—
and taps its bright foot in time to keep from dozing.

Author's Note: Firenza, Italy, birthplace of the Renaissance, remains a city of casual elegance. From the heights of the Fortress Bellevedere, Florence lies, rich and red-roofed, to the north across the River Arno. It was a month of drought when police cars with sirens were escorting water tankers through town, yet the people lived their lives intact and washed clothes in the fountains.

Margaret Mantle

MAXWELL STREET

The street is dying.
The sun pulls wet exhausted air
from the gutters where scraps of garbage
drown in dirty water.
Broken buildings lean and tremble.
Hungry creatures forage in hallways.

This is where they came
in their thousands, generations of them,
old men and women and babies,
skinny young eager men holding their breath
and jumping off the dock at Ellis Island
headlong into America.

Promises loud in their ears brought them to Chicago,
to Maxwell Street and the market
where they opened their battered suitcases,
borrowed pushcarts, set up trestle tables
piled with watches, socks, bits of bicycles,
all the minutiae of urban living sold for a song, or less—
a snatch of sound, a single trumpet note
from a black bluesman standing on a crate.

Maxwell Street,
Chicago in its urgent, early incarnation,
opportunity a word to tangle foreign tongues,
its promise, though, clear as the lighthouse beacon
swinging its shaft of light across Lake Michigan.

The blues was born again here,
singing the world's heart full of longing,
loss, resignation.
Nations met and mixed
and became a family, a city, became Chicago
on Sunday morning living, dealing,
swift as swallows—
"we cheat you fair,"
shouts and laughter and
the smell of onions from Jim's hot dog stand
sashaying up the street.

Parking lots and college dorms go up
and sanitation trucks sidle past with averted eyes.
But the people of Maxwell Street have been around longer
and seen more and sung and suffered with more passion
than the city fathers and seem not to hear
the death cart's clanging bell.

Their world has shrunk to a city block,
perhaps, but they can fit a world into that space.
Tourists still come and are not disappointed:
They see the street wake up on Sunday morning
as the folks for whom the dilapidated remnants
of this place still mean a room out of the cold
emerge from drab doorways, nod to curious cameras.

On the corner of Maxwell and Halstead
Jumping Willie Cox sweats and rejoices
to the band's pounding beat.
Huge, sweet-faced, Jimmie Lee Robinson,
silver spurs on his boots,
pauses a moment for a photograph,
then takes his guitar and mounts the makeshift stage
to sing the song of Maxwell Street.

It's Sunday morning,
and the people of the dying street
dance in the gutters,
comfort the broken buildings with music,
relive their past
defiantly
here on the corner
where the street still lives.

Author's Note: The Maxwell Street Market was once Chicago's most diverse and vibrant working class commercial district, the port of entry for successive waves of immigrants since the Civil War era. The electric blues was born here. Today the market has been relocated, and a scant city block of the old district remains.

Tom McCarthy

PHNOM PENH STREET

Ruptured macadam tackled the motorbike
knocked the two boys down hard
the crash didn't kill them
land mine hadn't killed him either
but the boy with no legs
couldn't scamper out of the street.
From the curb his brother watched
a big white U.N. military truck drive
over him face down in the roadway
double axle huge rugged dual rear wheels.
        My editor in Hong Kong doesn't
        want to know about this.
        "Khmer Rouge, goddamn you, McCarthy.
        What about the bloody Khmer Rouge?"
        Camera idle, notebook empty
        but war stalked the noisy streets
        elegant, decayed Phnom Penh
        the present killing the future
        past triaged and bleeding to death.
        "Get out to Svay Leu, damn you.
        Interview the camp commander."
        The real war was outside
        the noodle shop during breakfast.
The truck suffered barely a bump
25 hulking sweating Canadian soldiers
battledress, black assault rifles, baby blue caps
two grim corpsmen mummified the corpse
with great wads of compress bandages
just to keep it all inside
then hoisted the dripping bundle
onto a high-wheeled wooden cart
drawn by a stout, mud–smeared water
buffalo, eyes wide wet red
big black nostrils flapping, breaths huffing
spooked by the smell of the cargo
the brother laughing and crying
riding the bent motorbike alongside.

"Find the family? I doubt we can."
Sergeants are trained to shrug,
regroup and move on.
"Likely the family'll find the U.N."
Sweat pulsed through his camouflage
and web gear, sturdy face slick.
"I hate it when it's kids." Eyes away.

"McCarthy, you dumb bastard, you
went to cover a war and came back
with photos of children and grandmas."

Author's Note: As a newspaper reporter in Cambodia, I witnessed the scene that became this poem.

Hallie Moore

ANDEAN SNAPSHOT

Washing bright wool caps
in the common stream
brown–faced Cuzco mothers,
hunchbacked with last winter's child,
twist to hear a flute's
breathless poetry
pulling llamas
from thin air,
up the path
to Sacsahuaman.

Author's Note: Sacsahuaman is an Incan fortress situated high in the Andes, above Cuzco, Peru, former capital of the Incan Empire. The stones in the wall are larger and even more impressive than those at Machu Picchu. Flocks of llamas are brought there to graze.

Maria Quinn

ON A PLANE FROM CUZCO

Silvia Tuco is nervous about the flight, her first.
She busies the air around us with friendly,
frenzied chatter, but in half Spanish–half Quechua
and I can barely understand the Spanish part.
She came to Cuzco by bus, and it took three days.
I help her with the strange confinement of a seat belt.
She cannot read and feels some need
to tell me and apologize.
But she can wash and iron and cook.
When I ask about children,
she writes their ages for me
with great care and concentration
on the palm of her hand, as anxious
to impress upon me her ability to write a number
as I to show the few words I know in Quechua.

Recall the Andean response to the mixed mystery
of the written word, that disembodied speech
that took sound out of the larynx
out of the air, out of their huacas,
how the early conquered ones told
of strangers who "spoke in some white cloths
as one person would speak to another,"
how Atahualpa's capture came when
he could not hear the voice of their
talking cloths and threw the Bible
from him to the floor. The doomed
Inca, who assumed they were born with
this sorcerer's hearing, asked a guard
to write the name of God on his thumb.
Only when illiterate Pizarro could not
hear the message with his eyes
did Atahualpa surmise it to be a skill acquired.

Her children went to school, she tells me.
Each and every one of them can read.

Knowing Stones

She begins to bless the ground and the sky
we are about to enter. She is bringing
to Lima a large blue bag full of bread
which will not fit under the seat.
When the stewardess takes it away
she is not sure what she did wrong
or if she'll ever see her *panes* again.

She looks puzzled studying visuals
in the pouch pamphlet *"Para Su Seguridad"*—
pictures of people jumping out of a plane,
putting a strange yellow mask over their faces.
I try to explain and tell her not to worry,
but she does. She worries and worries
the dark wrinkly skin of her face with one hand,
worries the stale, compressed air with the other.
She tries to chatter faster than her fears
until, across me out the window, she sees
Salcantay raising its white–haired countenance
above the clouds like an old friend standing up to greet her
from the center of an anonymous crowd.
This white writing high on a tablet
of grounded mountain she can read.
"Salcantay" she says in wistful reverence
as if greeting the Inca on his litter.
She knows where she is now and can close her eyes,
whispering something in Quechua to the high-minded mountain.

Author's Note: Quechua was the language spoken by the people of the Inca Empire and is still the mother tongue of most Andean indigenous people of Peru. The magnificent, snow–covered peak of Salcantay is visible from Machu Picchu.

Tyler Enfield

RIDING THE COFFIN

"Can I go up top?"
"*No hay problema,*"
he says without slowing down
as I reach around and up
for the roofrack, hoist
myself to the bus' dimpled crown.

Luggage jockeys for center,
nothing strapped down, men
splayed out on duffle bags
smoking harsh piquant cigarillos
in thin Andean air.

A boy clutches his lamb
close for fear of dropping
like the mountain road's sheer edge.

And the bus bounces on....

Magnificent views gasp back
at us and our peril en route—
gears grind; mud spits rooster tails
over the side as
I bump and shuffle
for a place to sit.

A kind man wiggles sideways
pointing me
with his smelly cigarillo
to a humble station.

Beside him is a coffin,
blonde and lacquered,
rattling in earnest.
I straddle my wooden perch,
knock twice, hear no response,
so ride the coffin
like a solemn rocketship
through blistering
beauty of perilous heights.

Author's Note: In my travels I often find chaos amidst simplicity, and, as in this poem from the Ande of Ecuador, simplicity that is shrouded in chaos.

Carolyne Wright

THE MIRACLE ROOM

The Kodaks focus on the ceiling,
a Baroque reliquary, doll factory
of arms and legs. Facsimiles
the grateful make of ghost limbs
raised from the dead, silver medals
from the mouths of infants
who weren't supposed to live.
Before and after photos, testimonies
scotch–taped for years to the wall.
The home–movie makers
check their light meters
and wonder what's held up the tour bus.
They don't notice the little girl
who comes in through the side door
without a face.
They don't see her cross herself,
dip her fingers in holy water
with coupons from the Bahia Hilton
floating on its surface.
No one notices her slide
along the wall, finding her way
with the help of plaster hands
that catch hold of hers.
The charter group doesn't know
she's lighting a candle, kneeling
before Our Lord of Facelessness,
Our Lord of Bomfim.

They can't see the black madonnas
in their sea–froth lace
nod from the altars,
raise carved hands in blessing.
Not even the Cooks Tour guides
reciting from the souvenir brochures
glance over to see her rise,
blink, sneeze once, press fingers
to the deep rose of her mouth,
and skip out the chapel door,
swinging a mask
from which the features
have been erased.

Author's Note: In São Salvador de Bahia, Nosso Senhor de Bomfim, the most popular of Bahia's many churches, is famed for its colonial Baroque architecture and for the healing power claimed for its namesake, Our Lord of Bomfim. The faithful have filled several rooms off the high altar with relics and mementos of miraculous cures, especially of physical deformities.

Christopher Conlon

THE BALLROOM

She is the perfect image of a rag doll
I saw when I was a child, in a trash can,
dirty, ripped, abandoned:
here in the Kalahari is that same
doll, maybe five, eyes huge, legs
white with desert dust.
Ke kopa madi, sir, *ke kopa madi.*

Money: I shake my head no, no *madi:*
try to move on. But she stares at me,
suddenly transfixed.
No longer begging. Her eyes
wider than before.

My sunglasses:

I crouch down,
she approaches me, nose to nose,
tattered, filthy, she stares at me,
at herself.
Her hand moves to her chin
and she says *Oh,* in a tiny,
surprised voice. She rubs away
the dried spittle there.

Then she turns and,
whitened heels kicking up dust
like marble, dances away,
dignified, satisfied,
a tiny queen
in an endless ballroom.

Author's Note: An incident from my Peace Corps village of Tsabong, in southwestern Botswana. The little girl speaks in Setswana, the native language of the country; her words translate literally as "I want money" (though the statement is less rude in Setswana than it sounds in English).

David Radavich

EGYPTIAN TIME

Impossible! A giant horse
dancing through the hotel lobby
with a brass band, throwing out coins.

The bride comes after
her flowered accomplices,
and then the groom, a bit red-faced,
with taunting friends screaming
to join, to join, to sing,
to dance, to play.

Tired and not young,
heavy with witnessing, late
beyond years—
of course we do.

Some with cameras,
some with their own red feet,
the trinkets aside,
real coins, gaped smiles,

and the abandon
of a horse on four human legs
leaping beyond all check–out counters,
porters, maitre d's, sofas,
chairs, beyond tourist and native,
Arab, Christian, Muslim,
brown or red, tired or young—

to follow a music so raucous
and riveting, so wed of all catching life
we cannot deny the trumpets,
pretend, unjoin, or fail to snake along,
chanting the love–night on.

Author's Note: Based on an encounter in the lobby of the Cecil Hotel in Alexandria, this poem evokes the magical exuberance of Egyptian ritual and juxtaposes social customs and assumptions.

John Dickson
ECHOES OF A NATIVE LAND

Tell us about Bulgarian weddings,
how the old men sigh for nights that have gone
and women weep for their own disenchantment
as confident bride and wine-eyed groom
are joined until death does whatever it does.
How she, like brides the world over,
though somewhat biased by love, of course,
is ready for ruling and being ruled
and he stands beside her forsaking all others
but dreaming their faces, one by one.
Then the violins and the young girls singing
and mountains of food served by bountiful women—
Turkish halva and baklava
blending with the rose-oil air.

And tell us how sometimes a bride is stolen
by one who must have either her or death
and to hell with her several murderous brothers
who search the hills for his hidden cave.
Or how often friends get the groom so drunk
that he spends the night as part of the floor.
Or they carry him off to a nearby hill
and gag him and leave him tied to a tree
where he watches the light in his new wife's window
till almost dawn, when it finally goes out.

Or if he outwits or outfights them all,
tell how he carries his bride upstairs
and later that night sounds a trumpet blast
as he drapes their bedsheet from the window
to proudly display its patches of blood.
And the men with history in their faces
and women, unchanged for a thousand years
tell how then they stop dancing their dances
and shout their cheers and dwindle away
through fields of roses, through valleys of roses
that cling to the heat of the summer night.

Author's Note: Studying Bulgarian in the service during World War II, I paid special attention to the stories the Bulgarian teachers told of their homeland.

Don Schofield

ISLAND DANCE

An old man in black
leads the snaking dancers. Two steps up.
One back.
          And the whole village follows. Three hours.
Four hours. Not you,
          visitor, watcher,
with men at wine. Tired wives.
Children asleep across folding chairs.
Fluorescent lights.

Time was, the old man sings, *Zeus*
stepped to in the body of a bull. Muscles. Breath.
Danced into the knife. Left these steps and gold
coins on the virgin's necks, dowries worn
with downcast eyes. Two to front. One to back.

Thoughts descend. Five hours. Six.
To smoke and gilt. Where Snake
has wings hard round St. George.
Hammered blood in hammered dust.
Two steps up. One back.
          —The young men
won't wait. Blast of flute.
No, sing the old, *No, not yet!*
          They leap.
Slap boots. Slap thighs, *Opah!* then go
out from the train. Whirl the dancers past despair.
Make it clear. Snake is here!
          Waking wives and children,
even you, eyes on fire as morning light
comes through the fluorescent glare—
          You're with them now, the whole island
swaying home at dawn,
arm in arm up whitewashed stairs.

Author's Note: The village of Olymbos, on the remote island of Karpathos, is known for its strong adherence to traditional Greek ways. During the last night of Mardi Gras, the village holds a community dance in which everyone, dressed in traditional costume, (which some wear all year round) dances at an excruciatingly slow, hypnotic pace until, just before dawn, they burst into what seems a dizzyingly frenetic rhythm as they leave the public hall and dance on off to their homes.

Ashley Mace Havird

MOSAIC

No ozone at this height.
Just light, Olympian,
pouring from the cobalt bottle
of Cretan sky—
pouring onto the bleached altar of Lappa.

Rough Guide drew me, scavenging,
to this mountain village—
to the loose fence of chicken wire
around the mosaic floor—
inlaid Madonna too dull, nearly,
to distinguish.

A young man—he is striking—
works the puzzle.
No other life signs—
not even the usual skeletal cat.
"Byzantine?" I smile. Repeat,
again smile.

He does not hear—
no, will not hear.
He refuses to see me.

I stalk the crumbling alley
to an arched doorway
whose massive boards have rotted
a wormhole.
My eye absorbs the glare
of a roofless room
where fissured *pithoi* of Minoan design
flank a worn stone lion—Venetian.
The dust of ruins built
upon ruins. This is no place
for mortals.

In panic, in something like
snow-blindness,
I face the double axe-head of the sun.

A thick black shape—a widow—
punctuates the white.
Shuffling past with a pail of food
for her son, she levels me
with her stare.
She sees what I am not.

You—feeder of men,
burier of men—only you exist here.
You may shelter your son only so long
before the pattern of his cells
fragments
like the tile in his fading hands—
before, like me,
like your ghost-husband sitting
hunched outside the *kafeneion*
he is a shell of salt.

You are shielded by your purpose,
made goddess by your grief.

Author's Note: Ancient Lappa, southwest of Rethymnon, was in its time the most important city in this part—the "waist"—of Crete. First settled in the Minoan era, Lappa was renowned for its citizens of valor, who held out against the Romans even after the fall of Knossos and other major strongholds. It was destroyed in 67 BC and rebuilt during the Byzantine Empire.

Joy E. Stocke

THE RUG DEALER

The rug dealer stands on stone
in the center of his shop
pointing to rugs, antique
dowries displayed on whitewashed walls.

Red, he says,
first you see red,
color of Crete,
like poppies in a field,
like blood.

The shop smells of wool and tobacco.
And the women?
He nods,
In each village she makes her own color red.

He straightens the sleeve
of his suede suit jacket.
A lion in his den.
You like, he says.

Yes, I like.
Rugs and blankets
in neat, bright piles.
I imagine women
opening veins,
bleeding into wool.

Katze, he says, sit,
and lays a rug across my knees,
wool cloth woven one hundred years before.

And the other colors,
lime and lemon and blue,
shades of mountain and sky
and sea.

From his desk
he withdraws a bottle, a glass
and offers me *raki*.
Tsikoudia.
Fire water.

If you drink too much, he says,
it will make you crazy,
you will lose your head.
But a little—

I sip.
It burns my throat,
shoots heat through
my veins.

Already, I am crazy
for the mountains, the sea, the rugs.
Crazy for the women
who capture the pulse of the island's heart
in looms.

The dealer lights a cigarette,
sits behind his desk.
He closes his eyes,
leans head against leather,
exhales a secret.

Curls of smoke rise above him
like letters in an alphabet
I cannot decipher.

He knows I am falling
falling in love with red
falling so swiftly
I think I can fly.

Author's Note: Crete, largest of the Greek Isles, is in the southern Aegean Sea between Africa, Asia, and Europe. The flat or kilim style of weaving which the women practice bears traces of all three cultures. While it is the women who gather the wool, spin, dye and turn it into carpets, it is the men who are the merchants. The men are shrewd businessmen, turning the sale of a carpet into a duel of wits. Many, however, also treat their carpets with a reverence befitting a lover.

Pearl Karrer

PRINTMAKING: WIPING AN INKED PLATE

My tarlatan pad, black as the skirts
of the old Greek woman driving
her donkey ahead of me on the road
to her mountain farm, collects
ink from the black gloss spread
across my zinc plate, leaving semicircular
sweeps in the surface shine. The woman's skirts

brush her black stockings, her black shoes
follow the dust of her donkey's hooves.
Around her head she has wound a long
black scarf like a turban, crossing
her nose and mouth to filter the dust, loose
end swirling down the back of her sweater.

The woman resists the sun. Ink drags
against my pad and hints of pewter
show through the ink like the silvery under–
sides of leaves on the olive trees

thrusting from rockbound terraces notched
in the steep grade of her village where nets
hammock the branches, their mesh black
as my tarlatan, not a fruit to be wasted;

or like glimpses of donkey gray between
mulberry shoots slung over his back.
He carries his fodder into a farmyard
toward a wire corral. Tethered goats show
interest and stir from a crabapple's shade.

Shooing chickens away, the woman
unstraps the shoots. She pauses to rest
on stones generations of her family have
wedged into walls and waves at me: the black
grooves in her palms merge with etched
lines come to life on my plate.

Author's Note: The scene is transported from the Taygetos Mountains in the southern Peloponnese, soutwest of Sparta, Greece to my printmaking studio in California.

Deborah Byrne

THE SPANISH BOYS AT THE HOTEL MANX

They prepare French dip sandwiches
for exhausted whores on the fourth floor.
Take smoke breaks in the air shaft near the kitchen.

They listen to sounds and feel vibrations
from the honeymooners' room two stories up—
comment about the wife's nice ass.
No door on the bathroom,
they know the husband can see his wife pee
if he lies in bed just so and looks
into the mirror on the wall.

They chatter about the oily overweight bellhop
who sells them to men visiting the city
without their wives. One of the boys laughs,
tells the others about the bellhop's shrunken *cahones*
caused by childhood mumps. They look down at their laps,
laugh madly like a *padre* taken up by a bell rope.

They walk the Tenderloin Friday and Saturday nights
in heels so high pain rolls in their backs.
Their *all the way home toes* hurt and sometimes bleed.
The wigs make their scalps itch and smell—
and the dresses, too tight, always too tight.

They hold hands and talk about *paella,* the way an Auntie makes it
with saffron from the crocusses she sprinkles with rain water
when the moon has moved between the two hills
above the crayfish stream where an Uncle first kissed her.
They know the stars will hold their secrets
and they'll marry girls taught by nuns to sit straight,
brush their hair a hundred strokes each night,
and only look when not being looked at.

Knowing Stones

When they're old, they'll sit
in parched plazas near fountains
filled with rasping locust leaves,
drinking wine made from vineyards planted by ancestors
who never had to leave the land.
They'll look at boys who walk by—
especially ones who've just come back.
They'll know the look in their eyes—
so innocent they believe only the stars
know where they've been.

Author's Note: At this seedy hotel in the Tenderloin district of San Francisco, the Spanish boys would fix me paella and tell me about how lonely they were for their country. Later I would see them moonlighting; they were stunning in flamboyant costumes. Their moonlighting was what got them home quicker—to ancestral lands, family and friends.

John Gilgun

ALCHEMIST MICHAEL SENDIVOGIUS CONDUCTS A TOUR OF PRAGUE

" Quelles bizarrreries ne trouve–t–on pas dans une grande ville, quand on sait se promener et regarder?" —Charles Baudelaire

If the red–headed hippie with the ponytail,
kissing his girl on Charles Bridge
in the sandstone shadow of Saint Adelbert,
sprouts wings and joins the giddy swans
wheeling over Kampa Island,
there is nothing surprising in this.
The sun shines, having no alternative,
on the mundane city of Prague.
   If the large brown animal
   sleeping under the forsythia bush
   in the early morning fog on Petrin Hill,
   resolves itself into the Golem,
   and if he spits out the *shem* and cries,
   "Am I to suffer always?"
   Don't be surprised.
   The moon shines, as it must,
   having no alternative,
   on the everyday city of Prague.
If Rabbi Loew's granddaughter,
working now as a waitress
at U Dragouna on Parlerova,
brings a rose on your plate
rather than the goulash and dumplings you ordered,
and you find Mr. Death grinning up at you
from a drop of dew on a petal of that rose,
don't be startled.
The planets revolve around the sun,
as they must, and Prague,
Prague is, as always, simply Prague.

Knowing Stones

> If the onion domes of the Church of Saint Onion,
> patron saint of Czech onion farmers,
> begins to emit the odor of onions
> and the odor pervades the city,
> disrupting traffic
> and inducing early labor in pregnant women,
> there's no reason to panic.
> It's just another day in Prague.

You have two hours to explore the city.
Be back on the bus promptly at five o'clock.
I've arranged to have it vanish at five-fifteen.

Author's Note: Michael Sendivogius came to Prague in 1590, promising to turn base metal to gold, restore youth, prevent death, and cure diseases. As alchemist he was part con man, part magician, part quack, part shaman, and part wonder worker.

Walter Bargen

FROM BOTSWANA TO ZANZIBAR

I.

Somehow we find ourselves a beginning.
Some days it takes thousands of miles
and someone else to recognize it.
Even then we may pass quickly
from city to city. In one market
dozens of burros crowd around
the only tree in the village,
their tethered heads all facing the trunk.
Like fallen leaves draped over their shoulders,
buyers wrapped in brown robes circle
the gray rumps. In a far corner,
which is only dusty air, a group
of men dressed in suits and ties gather
into their own small knot. No one knows
where they have come from or why they are
here; perhaps to sell another God or hurt
someone. Beyond the beaten earth
of the market, on the edge of the dry savanna,
under a dome of cloud-thatched sky,
in front of all that is ever home,
two sisters smile, eager to tell their story,
but it begins in another language, and for
a few coins they smile broadly for the camera.

II.

On a dirt road that barely remembers
a direction, that is really only a memory
of a destination, a teenage boy, his forehead
painted with a white down-turned arc
that echoes his brows and has the grace
of an ancient Etruscan helmet, stops
and rests on crutches, temporarily hobbled
by his rite of circumcision. He accompanies three
young girls, each with a baby. Around their
necks are disk necklaces, flat as rings
of Saturn that stretch to their shoulders
and spin off a universe of colors.
One baby balanced on her mother's hip
is blind in the right eye. There are days
on this plain as long and dark and permanent,
but they continue on and out of sight
toward some dusty center.

III.

There are pink horizons and flocks
of flamingoes that stretch as far.
Light interrupted only by dust.
There are calderas that circle
erupted worlds. Blood drunk from
the goblets of slashed rib cages.
Elephants tear down block buildings
looking for water; wrench pipes from
walls, plumbers with trunks. The empty
cattle corrals are five-feet-high tangles
of thorned acacia branches, centered on
the herder's dung-plastered hut. These are
the final acts of waiting for the rains.

Author's Note: The poem was inspired by a striking slide show of some friends who had recently returned from a trip along the east coast of Africa.

John Gilgun

MAC DONNCHADHA, TOUR GUIDE

Have Mac Donnchadha take out
his partial plate
and bring the jaunty cart to the docks
to wait

for the tourists
from Lisbon or Liverpool or Trieste
"Would y' be wantin' the tour?
It's five pounds and lasts an hour."

have him wear that tartan cap
and the black coat with the rip
in the sleeve and no lapels.
Have his hand shake with the palsy,

which he hasn't got,
but he fakes it
to get their sympathy.
Have him wear his shamrock tie.

When he gets them in the cart,
have him start
singing a traditional song
as they clop along.

Have him say it's in Gaelic,
though that's a trick.
He just babbles, makes it up,
as they go along. *Clop, clop.*

Gaelic! He doesn't know a word.
But he sure can sing like a mockingbird.
So they get hypnotized.
He has this one glass eye

And he fixes it on them
And they're gone.
I've seen it happen.
Have him rap

his whip *crack, crack*
against Nellie's big brown back
so the cart'll go fast as the wind.
That'll bring to mind

"Men who live at the back of the wind."
Have him wave the whip like a wand
at that point and say,
"Men like that don't live today.

But they once did, here on Inishmore.
I'll take you to their fort.
It's all part of my tour."
This may be more than they bargained for!

Have him talk about his dream
of a continent beyond ocean's stream,
where the Hyperboreans
wined and dined him

one winter's night
on whiskey distilled from starlight
and potatoes grown on the moon.
"We'll be at the fort soon."

They pass a cairn. They pass a cow.
The tourists are nodding off now.
Have him give the whip a final crack.
Have him tell them God's truth:

"None of you will be comin' back."

Author's Note: The Aran Islands off the west coast of Ireland, jutting out into the Atlantic, are almost totally barren of vegetation. The playwright John Synge found the essence of Ireland in the people here, all of whom spoke pure Gaelic in his day.

Richard Fammerée

EULOGIA

Above the vindicating sea, rising whitely
from the kitchen's cold-handled blessing, her pale
cardigan flaps its green gathering
to every field her husband remembers, forking
windrows of wheat into dry, neat breasts.
He is ancestor and self in that dust-driven moment
his red face meets the rude wind.

Alice blue school blouses slapping
at clouds and the church is white and the water
surrounding the forbidden tarnishes; her skin is forgiving
where the water is silver and the ruin black as a mask
and unapproachable.

*Above the weaving of their hair a branch is trembled
for a berry as the wind would in the blond, open field.*

*Where is the end room shuttered with indigo
branches? From this throne of vernal conceit, milk cold
and bloated, bearing the fallen spears of pine, spines upon spines
sprite green up above the rust and mossy stream and insect
clouds—*

Dear Mary, soon-to-be-forsaken, Protestant-fingered
wife, provider for the children, proceeds from the yellow
door of the new kitchen to the tiled hall. Her blind Jack
Russell, sausage pampered, rodent wristed, bounces
widely at a sensation of sullen sunlight among
the fuchsia, spins with the grin and abandon of the closely
protected. The green-glassed porch remains narrowly open—
but only to Jack.

A fire is lit in the television room. Down the long hall,
bending to the convalescent slope of the piebald
hill, she sweeps out each stale fire, sending anemic
wisps into a wind frantic for the sea.

*Leam of light draw near the writing in their salmon bodies
at the cloven rock, lichened and forever keening, streaming,
kneeling, beaded wet and aubergine: screens of golden
leaf set glowing*

the woolly sheep pounding nowhere
up the clover. That last light steels the partitioned
windows of Johnny Byrne's Couch & Four
and the contiguous stone chapel up to its cloistered
window and the priest's residence where Father Mahon
once slept for two weeks without a mattress, for *he* was
a just man, a generous man—not like this new cleric,
trained in England.
—*God help us. Imagine a theatrical society in Cullenglen.*
—*As if we hadn't enought nonsense—and especially with
the youth now—*
—*Well, one can see why the church is having her difficulties.
It all started with that Vatican II.*
—*I suppose he'll next be wanting to do away with the Blessed
Sacrament itself—*
—*God help us.*
—*Indeed.*

Dissembler, cast a furtive stance this side of the glass
in the hollow bellied banqueting room: the powder of ash
breaking upon the grating, the brown bindings
and green bindings of mildewing authors, the long,
low-handled swords impaled upon the papered wall,
the palest and finest portrait of Catherine O'Reilly—*Do you
take this fair Aisling— I do, I do*—as the light moves,

abandoning her again to the contemplative
twilight of 1914.

Cygnets amplify the sable and viridian,
insignia of faith, for the fading shall not be forgotten,
not here. This night they awaken to the ripple of Niamh's
mirror. Here is the bright field of their gathering,
and the shrill of the silence is the sound of their chorus,
the memory of an intonation, the little whistles
and green stories, their prayers we repeat
in the gethsemane of our hearts.

Twin cygnets, darlings of the water darkling,
what do you know beyond the reflection of the low stone bridge—

Author's Note: Each day is a primary metaphor. We awake in *Genesis* and close our eyes to *Revelations*. This is evident in the unmanicured tranquillity of Gaelic Ireland.

Elisavietta Ritchie

THEM

The leathered man hauling his mule,
the immigrant woman throwing slops at dogs,
the kid at billiards, his hands smelling
of fish or the scent of a girl...

This brutal blessed gap, as between two
arms of the harbor when even at low tide,
ice like dumped paving blocks,
it's dangerous to cross.

                    Certain nights
after too much sweet wine or poppyseed cake,
we dream their dreams. We do not mean to,
we cannot wake in time to shut them out.

With the long reach of dead lovers, they
grasp our sleeves, scratch our skin,
snatch our pillows, leave us naked
on mattresses stuffed with corn husks.

The funnel blast that calls them back
to dory, barge or ship, we hear
miles from any port.
                    And their blood

matches our own, the murk
of their minds and lives seeps
into ours, as we try to ford
the straits, cross the ice in time.

Author's Note: St. John's, Newfoundland with its small, dazzling harbor.

Water Flows over Our Knowing

Beyond archaeological excavations, waves lap the shore and distant time comes closer, then recedes. Water seems to inspire philosophical musings on the self-consciousness of the universe or the river-like flow of time and expanse of space. Yet it is now as it has always been, and acceptance washes over our desire to understand.

Water turns rock to sand and makes, in its receding, a peninsula of an island. It can have much to do with the wearing away of barriers and distinctions as well.

The sea, like the land, has its dream places that inspire universal delight. Sail away to some of its magical ports and bays.

Sharon Scholl

BERMUDA TRIANGLE

In yellow pools of ship's light
waves scurry by like creatures
fleeing toward the dark. Luminous
pinpoints of distant cities
lift and fall through troughs
of sea. We glide past
as though pulled by angled
strands of starlight.

The ship flows through the web
having learned its way
from an infinite regress
of sloops and galleons.
We stand, enchanted, at the rail,
fragments in the art of cloud
and sail, muted tones
in the song of wind and engines.

From the dark deck at midnight
I watch the firmament go by.
The light has come a zillion years
across the bent bridge of gravity.
It will go on a zillion more
and die exhausted
on the distant threshold
of worlds unthinkable.

I am the same carbon creature
as the stars. The universe and I
are stuff conscious of itself,
yet baffled by our common mystery.

I am sailing Westward
through the glittering transept
of the Southern Cross.
Where the universe is going,
I cannot determine.

Author's Note: We sail into that storied area of the Caribbean where exotic islands call snowbound tourists, and where we are linked to centuries of voyages plying wave and star.

Dale Sprowl

NINETY–EIGHT POINT SIX

Air and water and self all seem
the same temperature here
so one doesn't know where the body starts or ends
or where the world begins.
And eyes don't know if what they see is outside or
in the mind, what is dream and what is real
because mind is so low, so slow,
it flows back and forth like the South Pacific
waves on the sand.
And noses don't know which flower is where
because white ginger and tuberose,
plumeria and hibiscus
cascade through air everywhere.
And feeding abundant never ends
because wild grow the breadfruit and mango,
the guava, papaya and passion fruit.

What did Eve eat?
Here
she would need no seduction to take from the tree.

Author's Note: Moorea, Tahiti is an island of French Polynesia, a group of volcanic, mountainous islands with the abundant rainfall, luxuriant vegetation, and the warm, equable climate of the tropics.

Lynda Calabrese

EVEN IN THE WORST OF LIGHT

Leaving the narrow streets of Parguera,
we're anxious to see the mercury shine
of micro-organisms in the stirred waters.
Still I'm stunned by the glow
as two girls dive into the shadow,
turn splash to spark in the blackness.

We knew to visit the phosphorescent bay
on a moonless night and though tonight's light
is the worst for viewing,
this is our only evening
on the Caribbean side.

When our guide fills a bucket with bay water
and tells us to form a circle
to block the moon's glow
I'm aware that we'll board the plane
in the morning, our son will leave
for school, our daughter will plunge
back to her life and friends.

As we lean over the gallon together,
I watch our fingers ripple stars
that glint as we stand close as ever
scooping the silver light of our last night.

Author's Note: From Parguera, a small town at the southwest tip of Puerto Rico, overcrowded boats leave every hour after dark to take curious travelers to the phosphorescent bay. Eerie pale-green waters filled with billions of micro-organisms produce odd, silvery patterns as they're stirred by the boat's wake. It is best to see this phenomenon on a cloudy, moonless night.

Marilyn Zuckerman

PHOSPHORESCENT BAY: VIEQUES

"... cosmos, atoms, cells are our true contemporaries."
—Julia Kristeva

Carlos says, *What a night.*
See that raft of stars.
You think it's a cloud
but it's the Milky Way.
No moon
and everything in the bay glows
when touched or agitated.
We are all Midas.
Stars drift through me.
My dazzling hair drifts out,
fish dart,
trail long, luminescent scribbles.
I lift my glistening arm—
to ultramarine light.
Later,
those who have stayed behind
touch our bathing suits.
Drops of water fall.
Look, they say
diamonds   diamonds.

Author's Note: Separated from the southeast coast of Puerto Rico by about eight miles of sea, Vieques is an island whose last Taíno Indian chiefs fought to their death against Spanish Conquistadors in 1514. For six decades the U.S. Navy has been holding military exercises using live bombs and shells. Puerto Rican opposition and numerous protests have served to bring the practice into question.

Daniel Green

NIGHT VISION

Floating in a lagoon the black water
gives no reflection of the starless sky.
Suspended in a space without borders
the all–pervading dark is endless.

In the hush the boatman signals that
we reach over the gunwales.
Our wet hands come out gloved
in sparkling phosphorescence.

Now begins a lighted ripple as black
water breaks in the billow at the bow.
A heatless flame defines the waterline
extinguished by the lightless sea.

Back to shore we toss an incandescent
spray into the sky, returning
in a dance of water–sprites
to the music of soundless fireworks.

Author's Note: *Bahia Fosforescent,* Puerto Rico.

Alan Elyshevitz

LAPAKAHI, HAWAII

In pans of concave stone the Lapakahi
dried the ocean for its infinite salt.
From beach to hill the village filled
with surplus fish and sweet potato,
sugar cane and breadfruit.

Waiting for a signal from the sea,
fishermen played *konane* on a checkerboard slab
or tossed spears at banana stalks,
though most fell short and pierced the fertile soil.

By the light of *kukui* lamps,
elders sent hyperboles up in smoke—
folk tales, *leis* of vowels, halos
above the children's heads.

As days went by, the Lapakahi
heard a crunch of consonants beneath their feet,
as *Ku'ula,* the fishing god, feasted
on too great a share of the catch—
the wrong god at the wrong time—
for the freshwater wells had emptied
through the suddenly permeable world.

On the bluffs of Kohala the Lapakahi
prayed for just the right moon,
the phase of replenishment,
while *Ku'ula* devoured the last of the fish.

Spears now rest among the rocks,
and wind steals water forever from salt.

Author's Note: Over 600 years ago on the Kawaihae Coast of Hawaii, indigenous people established a prosperous community based on fishing and agriculture. It is believed that the lowering of the water table may have played a role in the abandonment of the village in the 19th century.

Karen Douglass

A TOURIST COUNTS ON STONE TO SAVE HER

She's traveled hard and is in ruins. She looks back
from the train, and the past lies before her. All rock is old.
If all great buildings root like trees, how deep does this

citadel push toward the core? The sea has withdrawn,
leaving behind its shell–shocked stones to plague her.
At Les Baux the wind spins the world and drives cold rain

sideways against her and her toward high cliffs along ramparts
harder than bodies. She has no right to be here,
no liberty, no brotherhood, no equality with rock. Nor

will the ancient mill shield her, its mouth open to the wind.
She is small, tilting away. One leap would
give her atoms back to their source, let sun draw up

the dust and rain her down, running to the valley of
the Rhône, gaining by water what might be lost by
flame. In the distance horses and the sea ride inward.

Author's Note: The day I was in Les Baux, a very old French village sitting high over a plain, the relentless rain added to the disorientation of being in another place, almost another era.

Margaret Mantle

MONT–SAINT–MICHEL

Upon this rock, the angel said,
you must build His church. But Aubert,
being busy, did not listen.
The third time the bishop did not listen
Michael, the archangel, summoned fire
into his fingertip, bored in the episcopal
skull a hole just wide enough to admit
a celestial message into a human mind.

Thus did Aubert, bishop of Avranches,
thirteen hundred years ago build on this rock
a shrine, holy to God and sacred to the monks
whose voices, if you listen better than the bishop,
you can hear at dawn in the cloisters
disguised as birdsong and the seeking hum of insects.

Then, through the years, wrapped round and about
like swaddling on a child, layered like icing
on a great ceremonial cake, rose vaults and arches,
stairways, hidden chapels, majestic halls
for the greeting of pilgrims, soaring Gothic spires.
And over it all, Michael, thrusting his mighty
golden arm into the watercolor skies over Normandy.

All the time, swift Channel tides
surged against the walls of Mont–Saint–Michel
and strange things happened. A traveler
stole a stone from the abbey and fell sick of the theft.
Others were cured by healing waters. Something unnatural
restrained a sinner's feet until, penitent and absolved,
he knew himself free to climb the holy mount.
Some were miracles of a gentler kind, as when
the willful tide stopped short and held its breath,
midwife to the young girl giving birth on the sand.

Today pilgrim and tourist,
often indistinguishable even to themselves,
toil side by side up massive staircases
to the abbey's spire.
Below, multi-tongued notices alert both to the tide's
inevitable patterns and the hour at which the water
will drown the parking lot. Then you must leave the mount
or risk the hunger of the sea ... unless, perhaps,
your reason for being there is significant enough
for the angel to still the tide once more
to give you time to see, to feel,
to birth a pure thought, a vision, poem, or prayer,
to leave your mark on the compliant sand
here on the holy Mount of Saint Michel.

Author's Note: Mont-Saint-Michel, built on a rock in the English Channel off the coast of Normandy, France, is a place that challenges the identity of the traveler. Years, lines, lives, and understandings blur. Rock, sand, and sea are one creation; architectural styles of centuries encompass and absorb each other; today's tide of commercialism is pushed back as the visitor climbs closer to the abbey church that crowns the mount. And along the way the tourist leaves the guidebook behind, the better to hear the echoes of prayers audible only to the ears of the pilgrim.

Floyd Skloot

DAWN AT SLIGO BAY

Here a sky boiled sapphire
from the sea is flecked apple
and carmine, surging where it
is shot through with bolts
of sun. The dark shore
and its claw of land stand
no chance against a dawn
drawn like this from earth's
royal core. This is a blue
so deep it mauls all light
and bursts white to the eye.

Now in the very last moment
Sligo Bay can hold daybreak
back, the cliff crumbles.
Its colors blend in a creamy
plunge the scored sea never
seems to notice. Near shore,
breakers thicken and gleam.

There is nothing smooth or still
about the way sunrise lures
mist and sheen from drenched
rocks and tames the tidal bulge.
This should be the dawn a man
sees when he believes himself
free of memory at last. Let it
wash over him like harsh ocean
wind and he will not turn away,
even when a woman whose face
glows golden in the growing light
waves a bonnet the same raven
black the night leaves behind.

Author's Note: My wife and I visited Yeats territory, Sligo in northwestern Ireland. Though it was moving for me to be there and to see the dawn, the poem took its primary inspiration from a painting called "The Violence of the Dawn," painted in 1951 by Jack B. Yeats, the poet's brother. He loved dawns; he collected them, saying "There are ten dawns I would see again—if I was able."

Lorraine Tolliver

CABO SAN LUCAS BAY

Here the continent finally
gives up in a long, thin strip
punctuated by a few startling rocks
standing hard against crowding seas.
At this tip, the flash of life
on this flash of a planet
congeals and reveals itself whitely.
The land sweeping north
deceives with sullen, dry death,
barely willing
to push up scrub brush.
But life works here,
rich as under bluegrass skies.
Here the spindly–legged beetle
with his foolish lurches,
a proud member in the line of life,
here, the old, old bones left in the rocks
that whip back the seas,
here the flesh of man's ancestors
that mulched and marbled the land,
and here the spirit of those creatures
that tumbled into private movement
in the sea and wandered out of it:
a spirit that roams the wind
and feels young and innocent
and is neither,
but is loaded with the colors of change
and the hourglass of pain,
riding along on loving and dying.

Knowing Stones

Here, at this tiptoe point
on the slim land,
here, where water, rock and sky
seem, somehow, free
from organic knowledge,
here, I scatter out
some unfinished and untended dreams
on the independent air,
knowing such air's long ability
to fold love, pain, and death
into its distant hospitality
and, through deep time
to bring forth again
a small dot, alive and new,
on this small dot of land
signeting a continent,
grand and blatant
in pulling life together
on the vertical tablet
of rock, sea, sand, and time.

Author's Note: At the tip of Mexico's Baja California lies Cabo San Lucas, surrounded by the Pacific Ocean, the Sea of Cortez and, to the north, barren dry scrub land that stretches on and on.

Maureen Micus Crisick
LA PAZ
for Rachel Sarah

A low moon bowl holds part of the sky.
I see in your eyes one who has entered
this life with thin paper sheets
to write down the curve of the moon,
the grief of pine dried by sun,
the blinking owl's home in the cactus hole,
and your love affair with the palm
whose fronds have touched your hair
and caused your fingers to open this day—
to tell us how the sparrow eats
crumbs from your hand,
how the dark spider follows
your scent from room to room.

He will not harm you
as these will not harm you:
the low–strumming guitar of a man whose
voice blends with crows,
the Mexican boy sweeping plums on the stairs,
the white alabaster stone which comes up
clean on the beach. Or the conch shell
which listens to your breathing,
its ear turned up in the sand.

Author's Note: La Paz is a town in Mexico where my daughter was living. The writing started with the natural landscape and leapt into exploration of the mother-daughter relationship, ultimately arriving at *"La Paz"* (the Peace).

Ann Sylvester

THE RIVER

Did I tell you there is a river behind the Western Wall? It is an Eastern Wall depending on which way you are looking. At any rate, it is called the Western Wall, and it is leaning, and people are leaning toward it. If you are very careful and you prop your ears against the stone wall, you can hear water running. It is an old river, and if you hold yourself long enough, it will run right through you to the ground, and remain inside you running as you run toward your plane, run around the world, travel to high mountains, or fast in the desert. The river will continue running. Wild monkeys may dance in trees above, or fight for the fruit of idols. A large golden monkey may smile leeringly at you through a window. Aged yellow tigers, like careful butterflies, may stroll through slow forests, and guides may show you the path of the righteous. You may go to Kilimanjaro, Sharm El Sheikh, and Varanasi. You may pause under the Bohdi tree, reflect near a lily pond in the rain, where maroon–robed men meditate. You may enter the second floor of a brick building and discover a place where a man fills a room with blue light. You may find yourself in dark caves, and underground metal rooms. You may hear the wail of sirens. You may remember the sound of shattering glass, images of barbed wire and gray days. Ravage and rage may pour beside you in a rain of signs and trembling. Your neighbors and dinner companions may riot beside you.

In the river running through you, alive and colorful, you will hear stories. Now you may think that you will hear stories of who begot so and so, or the time when he lay down, lay himself down for a long... or the time he jumped, he jumped so high that... Actually, what you will hear ... Listen carefully, do you hear it?

The sound of ancient fish, the rustle of large ram's horns in the thicket. (A mesh of color mixed with dry leaves). The struggle of horns against the mass of branches, above the river. The sound of old water and sand. The old current, steadfast, dragging old stones, grinding away memory with a song.

Author's Note: The location of the poem is Jerusalem, Israel and many other places, geographical and internal.

Linda Casebeer

THROUGH BREEZES OF CHANTA PALMS

On the bird continent, it begins
in the low gurgle that throbs like sounds
from the throat of a frog, then twists
from water into song, waits.
Begins again to punctuate early
morning mists: the call of the ora pendula.
And it continues in turquoise, trogons
feeding on termites nested in mud,
the iridescence of a spangled cotinga,
high in the canopy. In the way
the aura of gold and turquoise flash
through breezes of chanta palms.
And palms. And palms.
The needled chimbera palm's
poisonous prick of my finger.
In the canopy's lavender jacaranda
blossoms scattered on the floor
under aerial roots dangling down
around the lania, everywhere
the twisted vines of our lives.
In the retinal blue after-image
of the brilliant morpho butterfly.
In the colpa where the apes and deer
slip down to drink in the dark
while the white saintwood gleams
in the moonlight. In the water's
breadth. In its myth. And more
than the shimmer of water or bird
or myth, in the ever-present heat
and moisture that overwhelm
and saturate moment by moment,
until the body, limp and satiated,
can imagine no other source:
this is how the Amazon claims us.

Author's Note: Rainforests of the Peruvian Amazon River are dense, humid, and enormously diverse.

Linda Casebeer

THE KILLING JAR

Bright blue grace flutters over
silt-colored rivers. Do not leave
the path to follow what flutters, since
in the clutter of large leaves and vines,
serpents move underfoot
like the first stirrings of desire.
At fifteen I followed what fluttered,
a catcher of things, net in one hand,
fingers of the other curled around
a Mason jar, daydreaming
about how to grow bigger
breasts and straighter hair.
Ignoring courtship
and other rituals, biology
taught us to classify lepidoptera.
To construct a killing jar:
soak cotton in carbon tetrachloride,
trace cardboard circles,
punch holes to allow the vapors
to rise, to still the flutter
of wings quickly, to leave intact
bright scales.
To use a spreading board
to reveal the beauty of underwings,
revelations of desire as clear
as the glass of the killing jar.

Author's Note: The "bright blue grace" referred to is the blue morpho butterfly. The first time I saw one in the Peruvian Amazon rainforest was a magical experience.

Linda Casebeer

TREE TOPS

We reach them by a series of ladders.
There is no stair to the canopy's birds.
Ladders loom close to tree trunks,
bridges suspended between them
like tasseled Peruvian hammocks.

These cabled Amazon bridges
sway the way I remember the suspension
bridge at Lookout Mountain
where you can look out over seven
states. If you look out.

This was how I learned fear from
my mother, when I watched her at the top
of the mountain: she, pale and shaking,
clutching her stomach.
Never look down she would say.

I remember the times she gripped
the steering wheel of the station wagon,
gritting her teeth as she drove over high
bridges, her gaze locked onto the middle
strip of pavement. *Never look down.*

What can we be looking for as we sway
in the tops of hundred foot tall trees,
in the late afternoon's mosquitoes,
in the smell of rot and fungi growing,
among birds gathering at dusk in still air?

Author's Note: In the primary rainforest of the Peruvian Amazon a walkway has been built for walking high in the forest's canopy.

Deanne Bayer

THE ARCTIC CYCLE

While world asymmetrically
turns, the Pole
stands still—the Arctic winter
is as close as we care to get
to eternity. In this land
of locked time, inhaling
begets fossils
and dreaming
takes on a dimension
more tangible
than reality.

We have no record
of how long it takes
to circumnavigate
the Circle. No one of us
has tried—the cold grows claws
like Polar bears scratching
at the residue of remembrance
we clench in ungloved fingers
venerating the sear
of frost, all we have left to imprint
past affiliation with heat.

Here, where we can hold
our breath
in our hands, minutes
fatten by digesting dreams

so that in this panorama
of interminable
space and time
for dreaming, the winter nightmare
is not the Calibans
that may haunt
our dark—the winter nightmare
is running out of dreams.

Author's Note: The poem was inspired by a fascination with the Arctic as a metaphor for an emotional landscape, and the belief that not even Caliban, the monster-like character from Shakespeare's allegorical "The Tempest", is as fearful as losing our ability to dream.

We Take the Dead Along or Meet Them There

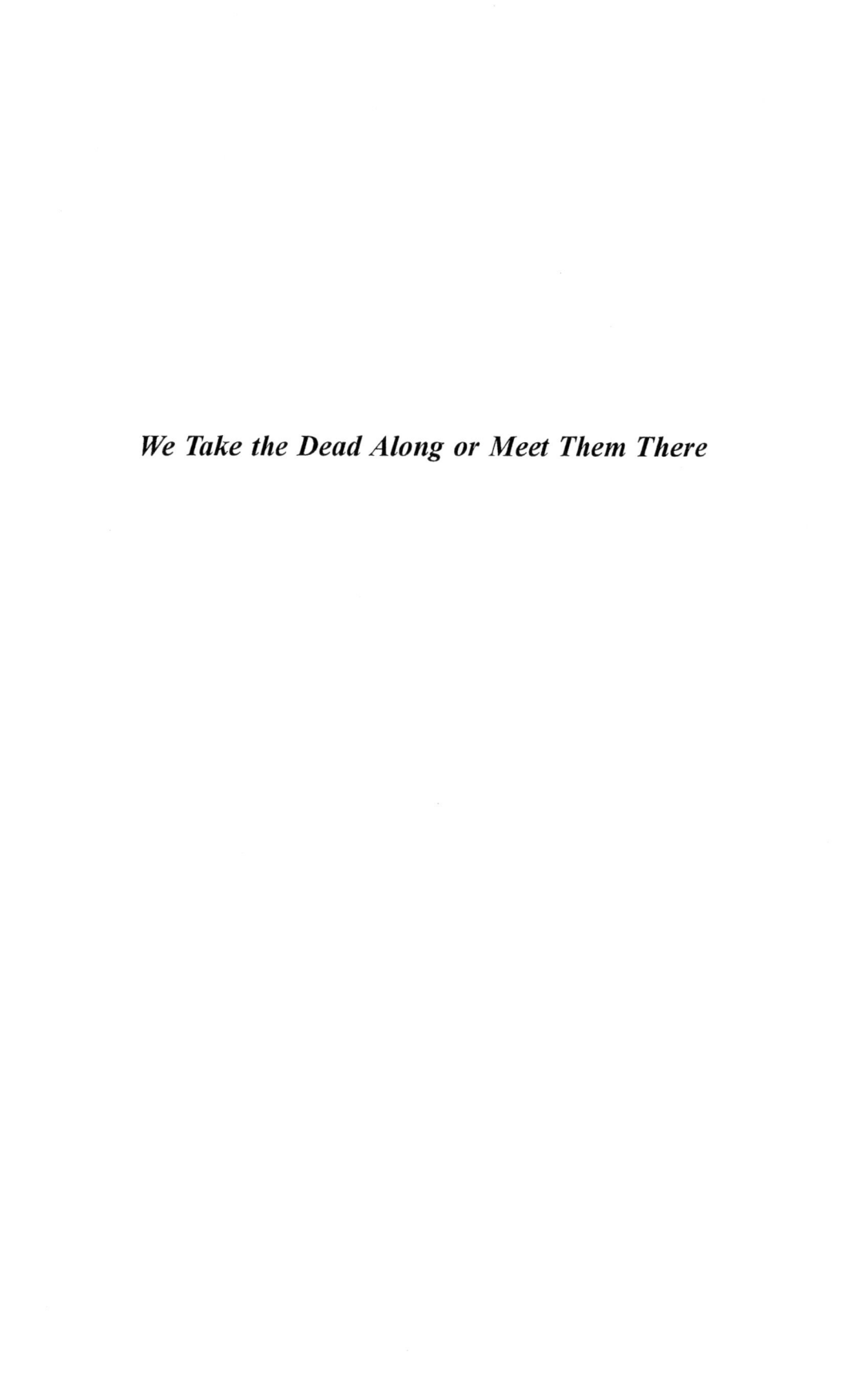

Like the old gods of a region, the dead want to be remembered. Since they are always with us, asking that their work on the earth be acknowledged and their unfinished projects be completed, the vulnerability of being a stranger renders a traveler even more receptive to them.

We see on passing strangers the faces of departed loved ones, recall the vocations of our grandparents, speculate in graveyards, contemplate, in catacombs, the macabre beauty of kaleidoscopic bones. The traveler may come to realize that he is not alone, but embodies his ancestors and provides them with a living link to earth.

These poems give us vivid and powerful images of the juxtaposition of life and death around the world.

Susan Terris

ON SEEING THE DEAD WALK

People walk the streets disguised as ones
I've lost, daylight mediums
who channel the disappeared to consciousness.
Yesterday, I saw Maria and last week
on the altiplano—Cara, then Aldo.

When Maria turned, she had no freckles.
Cara was too dark, and Aldo's eyes
weren't ball–bearing blue,
yet these friends reweave in daily murals.
Consider it personal archaeology:

to define myself by calling up the dead.

In Inca Skies, rainbows are two-headed serpents
and the Milky Way is a celestial river
rising. From it, the dead wade,
offer fresh–cut reed as proof they endure.
In Sucre where we star–gazed,

the graveyard arch said: HODIE MIHI
CRAS TIBI—TODAY ME, TOMORROW YOU.
My friends shadow me,
but they stay young, so I weft them
to strengthen old warp.

Author's Note: Sucre was the ancient capital of Bolivia. In the 18th century, because of active silver mining in nearby Potosi, Sucre was a sophisticated city even larger than Paris. The old arch over the entrance to the cemetery has its inscription in Latin, one of the languages familiar to educated citizens of colonial Bolivia.

Leza Lowitz

THE SEAMSTRESS

At the ceremony where old needles,
bodies broken in service,
are buried in the soft white tofu pillow
I think suddenly of my mother's mother
first in the ship from Ludsk
then in the tenement on the Lower East Side
where she sat over her sewing machine
pulling each piece of fabric
mute through its rusted tongue.
For years I haven't thought of her
until now, when this prayer—
an unlikely Buddhist mass—
stitches up the run in that old stocking Time
here in Tokyo, my Ellis Island of the mind.

Author's Note: *Hari–Kuyo* is the Buddhist mass for the year's broken sewing needles, held on February 8th of every year at Senso-ji temple in Asakusa, Tokyo. The needles are believed to have given up their lives in service of the seamstresses' craft.

Carol Kanter

TRAVELOGUE AT GLACIER BAY

The small boat bravely
rumbles me out into the salt wind.
Light mists skitter,
shroud and unmask the views.
Nearby, porpoises play
with the bow, the wake, each other.
Whales keep their distance
whole families, a megapod, meet
in the breach,
Sea otters scull on their backs,
preen, cock their heads forward
to look where they have been.
Puffins, plain and horned,
bob, fill their wedge beaks
with fish—lined up in one neat layer
head to tail to head.
Mergansers edge ice mountains
waiting for them to crack,
resound like gunshot,
a starter pistol cue: Dive!
for shrimp roused up
as the glacier calves—delivering
swells that rock my boat.

And I skim backward
a handful of years, listen again
to my dad as he, awe–struck,
re–lived this momentous,
monumental scene
from the last trip he ever took—
the sight of unmoored
snow–white cliffs shearing off,
whole walls crashing,
splashing down into the sea,

a sudden geyser spewing foam
high into misty air
before it settles, quiets,
bares large floating blocks
of jagged, dangerous
new dead ice.
But, Dad, you forgot to tell
about the gunshot crack—
so shocking loud and puzzling:
Why did you shy from this
final metaphor of fair warning,
when you knew
already you'd begun to die?

Author's Note: If you take one of the small boats in Alaska's Glacier Bay you can see the ice mountains up close and personal.

John Knoepfle

notes from a journey

basho in the deep north of his soul
went home after his mother died
it was a full year later
and he was a gaunt man beaten by wind

he could not find
her small garden
now a shadow of herbs
she grew outside her bedroom window

his brothers wrinkled in their smiles
gave him a lock of her hair
they had kept for him
the white hair of his mother

and he had tears for her then
and for those brothers
all bending he knew
as he himself was

under the cold hand of time

Author's Note: Derived from *The Narrow Road to the Deep North,* a beautiful work by Basho, one of the great Japanese haiku poets.

Gary Mex Glazner

THE ORACLE OF DELPHI

The only ones left to answer any questions
are the rocks.
They know the yellow of the sun's sour heat.
What trees drink. How the empty seats
of the theater clamor for an audience.
The immovable rocks are spewing
forth their nonsense; I'll interpret.
They are disgusted by the lack of air.
They await the rebirth of breath.
They look down to the sea,
to Byron's grave, his heart buried far
from his body.
The rocks fill the empty cavity of his chest.
Sounding voices
of the nations of the world.
They understand every tongue.
Answer with the years of the earth.
The rocks care not for nations.
They speak the silence between languages.
The Oracle is gone.
She has left the rocks as prophets.
To tell us what is blood.
What is this flow, this beat inside.
Daring us to come out, to
feel the sun's warm knowledge.
Tell me your secret, is it the fire of stars?
Tell me your story, how quiet is stone?
Do the mountains know how much you
want to sleep with them?
Sweeping away the dirt from your grave,
I touch the stone above your bones.
I smell the orange scent of
death rising from your tomb flowers.
In the valley above Delphi,
you came back to die.
You loved the fabric of this land.
Made your own cloth of light.
Wove the myths to hold beauty.
to hold love.

Here, have a bite of this pomegranate.
You are not the Oracle,
although your seed is buried with her.
I have so many questions,
if I started to ask, I would
also lie down forever.
Live as these rocks live.
See the future they see.

Author's Note: Angelos Sikelianos is one of Greece's best loved modern poets. In the 1920s, Angelos and Eva Sikelianos recreated the Delphi Games, including performances of dance and poetry. Eva wove the costumes. I refer to her and her grave site at the end of the poem.
The prophecies of the Oracle were transmitted as poetry.

Richard Fammerée

EVORA (A Song)

In Evora there is a church
and the church was once a mosque
and the mosque was once a church
and the church was once a temple in the time of the Romans

Behind the altar there is a false tomb
and beneath a Christian name there are thousands of years
of roots writhing through stone
and water echoes up vertebrae which must have been steps
and its light is the juice of emeralds

Now, consider the well that is my throat
and the pool that is my chest

What does one do when a well has been capped
for so many generations?
Is water safe in the stomach?

How did I become addicted to a self-imposed periphery,
its tithes, its prick and its poison?
Can all this be unlearned in one generation,
one season, one summer?

My grandfathers and grandmothers
and their grandparents meet for the first time in me
I carry them to familiar places
I am their hands, their thighs, their nose,
their eyes, their lips, their teeth, their tongue

Knowing Stones

How did I become addicted to a self-imposed periphery,
its tithes, its prick and its poison?
Can all this be unlearned in one generation,
one season, one summer?

I am the voice and the body now
and all that is closed will be opened
and all hurts will be repaired
and all that sleeps without dreaming will be green again

In Evora there is a church
and inside the church there is a tomb
and inside the tomb there is a cistern
and inside the cistern there is water
and its light is the juice of emeralds

Author's Note: At the confluence of the Atlantic and Mediterranean, I stand as a cathedral sustained by a diligent congregation of ancestors.

Enid Shomer

TO THE FIELD OF REEDS

Look now, the guide says, at the story
from the tomb of the scribe, Ani.

Accused of too studious a life, in the frieze
above my head Ani gains heaven because

his heart passed the test. But first, reclined
on a slant board, he's gutted and drained

and packed in natron to stop the rot.
The husks of two crocodiles and a pet

cat, all bound in linen, accompany him
to the Afterlife—not the stuffy room

they found him in, heaped up with booty,
but a small desk stocked with dyes

and inks and a pair of palm fans to sway
over his two ghosts—the one who'll stay

in his body, fingering the quill pen,
the barley and wine, and the one,

more like our souls, who'll wander far from home
as I do now in the British Museum

where I witness the trial of Ani's
heart: separately

preserved, placed on golden scales,
it's weighed against a feather to settle

his final fate. Will the two totter, equal
as dry leaves on a wave? Or must his heart be full

of feeling, heavy with passions, for Ani to cross
to the Field of Reeds?

But look! It rises, light
as a grain of pollen or this surprising thought—

that paradise measures not pain or duty or even love,
those trophies saved in the heart, but what we can give

up. In the last panel, beside Osiris' throne,
see how the vacant-hearted scribe takes to the divine,

conversing with the half-mad,
the half-animal gods?

Author's Note: Egyptians could not be admitted to the Field of Reeds, the Afterlife, unless properly mummified and outfitted. They then had to pass one final test: the heart, separately mummified, weighed on golden scales, had to be lighter than a feather.

Tom Roby

REQUIEM

Only with you
do I hold the hour's peace
recalling our poems
in the rainy Italian graveyard
bright with neverfalling
flows of flowers;
on the dry steps of the Bona's chapel
do I hear canticle birds
trade tunes with vesper bells
that clang out Catholic hymns
known to your youth;
do I watch replanters
water memories that slip past
formal oval portraits
to a grin reflected
in a glass of wine.

Only you said that time had come
to trade poetry for dinner,
just as my soft electric candles
began to cheer
our damp twilight;
then I remembered
how I hate to leave any place,
and you reminded me
we will have our turn
when we won't have to leave.

Author's Note: In the "Valley of the (preEtruscan) Camunians" in Northern Italy we stayed at Capo di Ponte to study the world's largest known concentration of petroglyphs. Here we found a cemetery with an unusual and elegant arrangement. In the center are the gravesites; on the sides are chapel tombs and rows of above-ground vaults, arranged six high, where mourners use ladders to place flowers in the top vases.

Deborah Byrne

AMARYLLIS

If you are young
And just married
Look where whale
Meets ocean
And gets into your eyes.
Remember Naked Ladies
Making pink
Among gravestones—
Contemplate these stones
Holding onto Portugese names,
As if they are chipped teeth
In smile laughing at a place
Where water skies
Beyond control.

As Naked Ladies tickle
The dead with their bulbs—
Feel the ground,
Take its pulse,
Push aside soil to steal
A Naked Lady that may
Or may not grow in the garden
Planted when the honey–
Moon is over.

Author's Note: In the graveyard above Mendocino, California, the marble markers had mostly Portuguese names—ship captains, wives who waited for them, family people mostly. In the beds of the graves grew Naked Lady Amaryllis, colossal pick trumpets atop lusty, long naked stems. Their pink was vibrant against chipped white sugaring stones, a cerulean sky meeting a gray-headed ocean beyond.

Richard Beban

WHAT THE HEART WEIGHS
(IN THE CATACOMBS, PARIS 1997)

Death is bones the color of leather,
death is a skull with sockets like lace.

We spiral down & down like a feather
caught in a column of air; we face
the walls that twist & tighten & stone
steps that refuse to echo our feet. We turn
& turn & dizzy we finally halt,
thirty meters below the Paris sun.

The air still & cold, Lord, so cold,
the gush of blood in each ear silenced.

We thread long narrow lanes to
visit the dead by the thousands,
freed of the weight of viscera, of love,
their long bones hollow save for
capillaries stilled to petrified foam.

My body hangs heavy from my shoulders,
a cape I wear of organs & flesh. My face
the flat stare of Renoir's woman
stunned on absinthe.

*

The Egyptians claimed at the moment of death
the heart was weighed in the underworld
by the goddess Ma'at against a feather of truth—
light hearts rose to heaven,
the heavy dropped to the deepest pit.

I think how much like gods our parents—
wounded gods inventing gods as clues
to their own fallibility. Cruel mother
once–removed
to stepmother or witch
so children can bear her split
as both source of life
& slayer.

Knowing Stones

& as adults, we learn we are split
many, many times, the way the seemingly solid
earth is cobbled
from massive plates gristly & moaning
at the faults. Our skulls only gradually
join, fissures fuse
to a solid dome of protective bone.

*

In French, earthquake is *tremblement
de terre*. Our "terror" comes
from the Greek, to tremble.
Those terrors that shake us
from sleep are the worst. We were so safe,
slept like Medea's children. Innocent
in dreams, we wake to her betrayal,
her truth: we are only fragile bones.

*

After hours, years, we rise
from the catacombs, free,
blink noonday sun like newborns,
cling to each other, touch
the simple joy of muscle
& flesh & heat of skin laid sweet
over these armatures of bone.

I love you more then
than I have ever loved
& know too, I must soon forget
or go mad.

Author's Note: My wife and I visited the catacombs on our honeymoon. These limestone caverns under the streets of Paris contain the bones, arranged in artistic tableaux, of six million dead, exhumed from suburban cemeteries as the city grew. The caverns were used as hiding places by the French Resistance in WWII, as the Nazis refused to go into the place.

Bill Yake

MICHAELSKIRCHE, VIENNA

At eleven the tombs are opened:
vaulted silent alleyways.
The loyal dead stay beneath
the sanctuary: a crowd
of coffins, leg bones neat
as cord wood.

They earn their keep.
Hand bones—commas heaped in corners,
ribs (as parentheses)
and backbones, each column
the articulated consonants
of hymns and morning vespers.

Vowels long gone, decayed to air.
Each ending with a sigh—an exhalation—
a small black dot, period.
The air gone out of another story.

Overhead the heels of women's shoes
click on sanctuary tiles:
rosary beads, abacus clacking,
markers or wires in old pool halls.

Fifteen schilling to the parish for the dead—
toll to breathe the air of tombs, fee to work
on the puzzle of devotion, tribute to read
in this library of bones. To divine
some other meaning than the holy church
intends.

Author's Note: In Vienna (Wien), Austria all gardens are formal; even in the cemeteries its birds sing classical themes; the animals in its museums are stuffed and dusty. The only wilderness here is that of the soul. In the late 80s I was directed to St. Michael's Church by my sister who was living in Vienna.

Lynore G. Banchoff

DIVISIONS

The mathematicians face each other
on a moon–splashed bastion
above the Danube divided city.
Silhouettes locked in theorems
block light trails and night sounds
rising from the bridges.

I watch from below
with my back to the Hilton
of glass–embedded stone
built around ruins of an ancient monastery
where the glitterati contemplate holy mysteries
with a raised glass at cocktail hour.

The hotel holds the chapel in a triune embrace,
on the open side, a planter forms an altar
under a Gothic ceiling arching into space.
Rain–washed night pours over me,
and my feet stand in a mirror of water
formed by graves along the floor.

A chill vibrates my body.
Who stands behind glass?
Who is the visitor,
and who the visited?

Author's Note: Several years before the Berlin Wall came down, I accompanied my mathematician husband on sabbatical in eastern and western Europe. In Budapest I was struck by co–existing dynamics: the contrast between the material and spiritual realms and the pursuit of abstract ideas in the presence of great physical beauty and a quiet, pervasive spiritual presence.

Paulette Roeske

THE BODY CAN ASCEND NO HIGHER

–Capuchin Catacombs, Palermo

Hung up on hooks,
they lean from their niches, these thousands,
each with something to show—
top hat, Count Dracula cloak,
Jesus beard, two blue eyes
dry as eggs. Someone
has planned this party,
rigged the monk with a broomstick spine,
the bride with breasts of straw.
In a high alcove, an unascribable breeze
lifts the veil from a seventeenth–century face
that mocks the old promise: *dust to dust.*

But how they tire of the dry
preserving air, immovable hand
falling short of what itch, the generations
trooping past arrayed in the dress of the times—
those mirrors they stare back at,
showing how the world has not changed,
chaining them to their lives
as they would have led them.

Author's Note: During the 17th–19th centuries, more than 8,000 bodies of wealthy citizens, clergy and children were interred in the catacombs at *Convento dei Cappuccini* in Palermo, Sicily, many of them mummified naturally by "the dry preserving air." Often elaborately adorned, they line the walls of the labyrinthine passages through which present-day friars lead guided tours.

Laurence Snydal

VISITING THE DEAD

I call on Napoleon. The deep well holds
Remains of the First Empire, surrounded
By the splendid dead of the France they founded,
Marshalled under gold leaf and marble folds.
Outside it rains. Inside, the mystery
Of death becomes a page of history.

Karl der Grosse lies in Aachen. I feel
The fluted stone above his body, stand
Before the triptych that once felt his hand,
See the silver that magnified his meal,
And try to understand how granite can
Contain the greatness that contained a man.

Deep in Vienna's heart the Hapsburgs sleep,
Cradled in caskets of cast iron and stone.
They slumber best who do not sleep alone
And cannot care whose company they keep.
I sit and sip melange until we meet
And marvel at the sunlight in the street.

Can we remember what must be buried?
I have seen Lenin lie like a wax doll
In a hushed chamber. Behind on the wall
Tablets mark the revolutionaried
Few whose bodies' proletarian presence
Reassures the workers and the peasants.

I'll have no such solemn end. I'll molder
Incognito, my bones becoming earth
Anonymous, anonymous as birth.
My body will decide to grow no older,
And people in their living rooms will see
No more than they have ever seen of me.

Author's Note: On two trips, one to Paris, Aachen, and Vienna and another to Moscow, I found the contrast between these four tombs to be indicative of the different cultures that produced them. The French glitter and glory; Charlemagne in a granite box; the wrought iron arabesques of the Hapsburgs down and under a busy Viennese street, and the solemn mausoleum where Lenin lies embalmed.

Bertha Rogers

THE BARBER SURGEON'S DEATH

On Avebury's night side,
beyond the double-circled stones,

swifts scissor the rainlight,
ring around Silbury Hill,

that old witch's teat.
To barrow-hallowed fields,

to ring shelters they turn;
they scythe the air

above toppled monoliths.
Did the barber surgeon have time,

before the shadow
came crashing, to wonder

why gods must be buried? (All
his coins, all his pocketed tools

could not save him.)
A church rose within the ring,

a sacrilege to standing stones.
The itinerant's ghost, returning

to the drama of his death,
hovers in the slow, stained light.

Earth's old woman stirs,
offers her passage breast.

Before how many altars
did the barber surgeon kneel?

How many savage wings
did he beseech

before the night discovered him?

Author's Note: Avebury is Britain's largest stone circle, erected around 2600 BC. In the Middle Age it was customary to bury or otherwise destroy the standing stones which were thought to be associate with pagan rites. Around 1320-25 a barber surgeon was crushed and buried by one of the stones as was engineered into a pit.

William Greenway

SELF–BURIAL

These feeble pilgrims trekked so far
to reach this chapel just to die,
dragging threadbare deaths across
the hills of half of Wales to lie,

the three of them together, underneath
the yews to make a row of moldy tombs.
Now the congregation's gone away,
leaving crumbled, roofless rooms.

The glazier and ropemaker sat and watched
the mason carve each narrow stone—
a cross of rope on top, the lattice look
of leaded glass, and then his own,

with lines like ribs, crossed hands, some rings.
And when they died he closed their eyes and laid
them down and covered them, then somehow pulled
on top of him the ton of slab he'd made,

a perfect fit, no fingers caught outside
to line like chicken bones a fox's den,
with nothing left beyond the graves
to body forth the deaths of private men.

I wonder how a man today
could die alone with friends, with grace,
with nothing crucial left undone,
no mess about the dying place,

just stones and vines so tangled, old,
they're gnarled as Michelangelo's,
those naked humans, twined and holding on
to one another as the oceans rose.

Over stiles and past the arks of barns,
the bishop visits once a year,
walking through the muddy fields to hold
a wafer out to pilgrims coming here,

like us, who'll bury friends, and old,
alone, our journey done, will go half–starved
to lie beneath the weight of stone,
the one we, all our lives, have carved.

Author's Note: Wales is covered in holy stones, cairns, crosses, markers, and dolmens, and it provided the stones for Stonehenge. The graves of "Self-Burial" are found on the pilgrim's route to St. David's Cathedral on the west coast of Wales.

Kate Gray

BURYING BABIES IN INDONESIA

On the island of Sulawesi, mothers
        with machetes cut tombs in tree trunks,
ebony, mahogany. In hibiscus they hollow a place for bodies
        of babies, dead from drinking water, river water
stagnating, soil saturated; nothing stays buried
        on land. They place small bodies upright
in graves carved in the heart of wood, lash bark doors
        shut with sashes until they seal, faint green lines mark
casket covers in trees. In the rainforests of Sulawesi
        trees sway in the hot breeze, each marked
with latchless doors. They rock small wooden hearts.

Author's Note: While traveling in Indonesia I learned that many of the 25,000 islands have too much water to keep the ground solid, too little clean water to drink. Nearly sixty per cent of the children die before age five.

James Doyle

THE WELL OF SACRIFICE

I.

Dawn rises in green, slow
light climbing from leaf
to leaf, white rain swelling
into drops on frond
and bark, descending layer
after layer through the air,
breaking into milky ripples
across the midnight
of the well. Trees bent
by heat admire their reflections
in the thick water. Insects
grind the blue vapor
rising from copal into tiny
circles and stars. Crevices
of limestone blossom
with snakes. Three figures
in turquoise flesh wait
on the temple steps for day
to wash the darkness
from their bones.

II.

As the sun curves
its petals over the sacred
cenote, a priest moves
to the edge with a flint
blade. The gold serpents
carved into the handle spiral
around each other again
and again as the knife
plunges toward the water
below. A lord strips
five matching rings of copper
from his fingers and lets them drop
with a gesture into the pool.

Knowing Stones

The air fills with falling
metal and stone. Miniature
bells with their sound
cut out, jade
necklaces, beads
of amber and crystal all
disappear like night
into the thick green folds
of the morning well.

III.

At the proper sign
from their lord, the three
persons, husband, wife, and child, will be hurled
into the air, their veins
carrying our blood, their skin
painted with the blue
flesh of our worship. They will dance
in the dark undertow
with the gods. The secrets
of the rain will weave
for them a tapestry
that tells the changing
seasons. When the sun
reaches the center
of the sky, we will part
the surface of the pool
with our eyes, reading
in every ripple the hieroglyph
of return. If the deep springs
that feed the well flow
with our prayers, our messengers
will rise again. Earth
will marry water
and we will see
all the graves of the burning year
blossom into harvests.

Author's Note: At the Sacred Cenote of Chichén Itzá, a Toltec–Maya site in the Yucatan, sacrifices took place at dawn over a thousand years ago. First the objects and then the people were thrown into the water to sway the rain god into granting a successful harvest.

Walter Bargen

THE CIVILIZED SACRIFICE

I have climbed the backs of gods too. It's not so
strange, dressed in heavy coat and boots, hat
pulled down to the eyebrows, cheeks windburnt,
gloved fingers numb, and each brief breath prayed

upon, each step thrown onto the loose altar of stone.
Blinded by the rising spires of light, I have looked
away as the unblemished blue sky splintered
in all directions. I have backed from the sheer

precipice, the infinite suddenly a fearful measure,
all the way down to tundra and the jagged maze of
granite, leaving only a crevice in which to cower.
I've lain on the steep slopes of night under spruce,

wrapped against rain and cold, and watched clouds
explode in my face as the stark boughs reached
then sagged back in a sweeping, resolute silence.
I was not shaken loose even by thunder

and lightning, unlike the small girl, named Juanita
by strangers. She tumbled a hundred yards down
Nevado Ampato peak, her whereabouts unquestioned
for five hundred years until a nearby volcano

began a festering eruption, thawing the slope.
Wrapped in her *illiclia* shawl woven in the ancient
Cuzco tradition, wearing a toucan– and parrot–feathered
headdress, her frozen fetal posture a last effort

at warmth above treeline amid ice fields, she was
left to address and redress for rain and maize, for
full vats of beer, plentiful llama herds, for
the civilized sacrifice, to be buried alive and wait

in private, as we all do to speak with our gods, hoping
to appease, to know, to secure the illusive cosmic
machinery, and in that last numb moment her left
hand gripped her dress for the intervening centuries.

Author's Note: When I read about the mummified remains of a young Inca girl who had been sac
ficed half–a–millennium ago in the Andes, I recalled my experiences hiking, mountain climbing, a
confronting the overwhelming god–like forces of nature.

Shelley Berc

THE MUMMY OF ACONCAGUA

In the freezer where he has lived since the mountain climbers found him at 18,000 feet in 1975, the five hundred year old child lies curled on the rubber baby mattress of pink and white sheep and ducks floating on clouds.

He lies on his side with a white cardboard band from the laundry around his head, keeping it in one piece.

The top of his skull missing, scooped out, like the Campo in Siena, where the horses run the Palio and the sky is the shape of an egg.

His hair, black, scattered sleep on pillow. There are seeds in his hair— five hundred year old seeds from the Andes.

His shape is fluid energy alive—but what kind of life? How could *this* ever have been flesh? Yet it has the most human peaceful spirit I've ever seen.

He still has some eye lashes left. They twitch in the wind of our eyes where he is dreaming. What would a five hundred year old child sacrifice be dreaming?

Surely he passed the summit of the mountain into the sky. That's where we'd find him if we could enter his dream, walking the cloud bridge that appeared when the priests left him with a bag of cooked beans and a golden llama for the journey.

He doesn't look cold, he looks happy, curled up as he is, lazy *n*. He looks like he's been traveling, rolling like a wheel over anything we could say about.

His mouth is open, no lips but shadow, as if he had just been kissing someone when they took the lips away.

His body is red, dark red inside and out. The priests painted him, then made him drink the pigment, so the experts say when they ask:

Did they do this before or after they reached the extreme cold in which the boy was to die? Did they kill him or did he die by himself from exposure?

Why would the gods of the sky want a child the color of blood; what does blood have to do with sky?

His teeth are white, though some red stained, too, and set like clouds in the mouth that is not there. If teeth are clouds, then in this equation, blood must be the mountains.

No eyes, no top of head. It is the absence of features that gives the impression of depth of vision.

Author's Note: I saw the mummy in Mendoza, an Andean Mountain town in Argentina where the archaeologist Juan Schobinger has an institute at the university there.

Altar Stones will Alter You

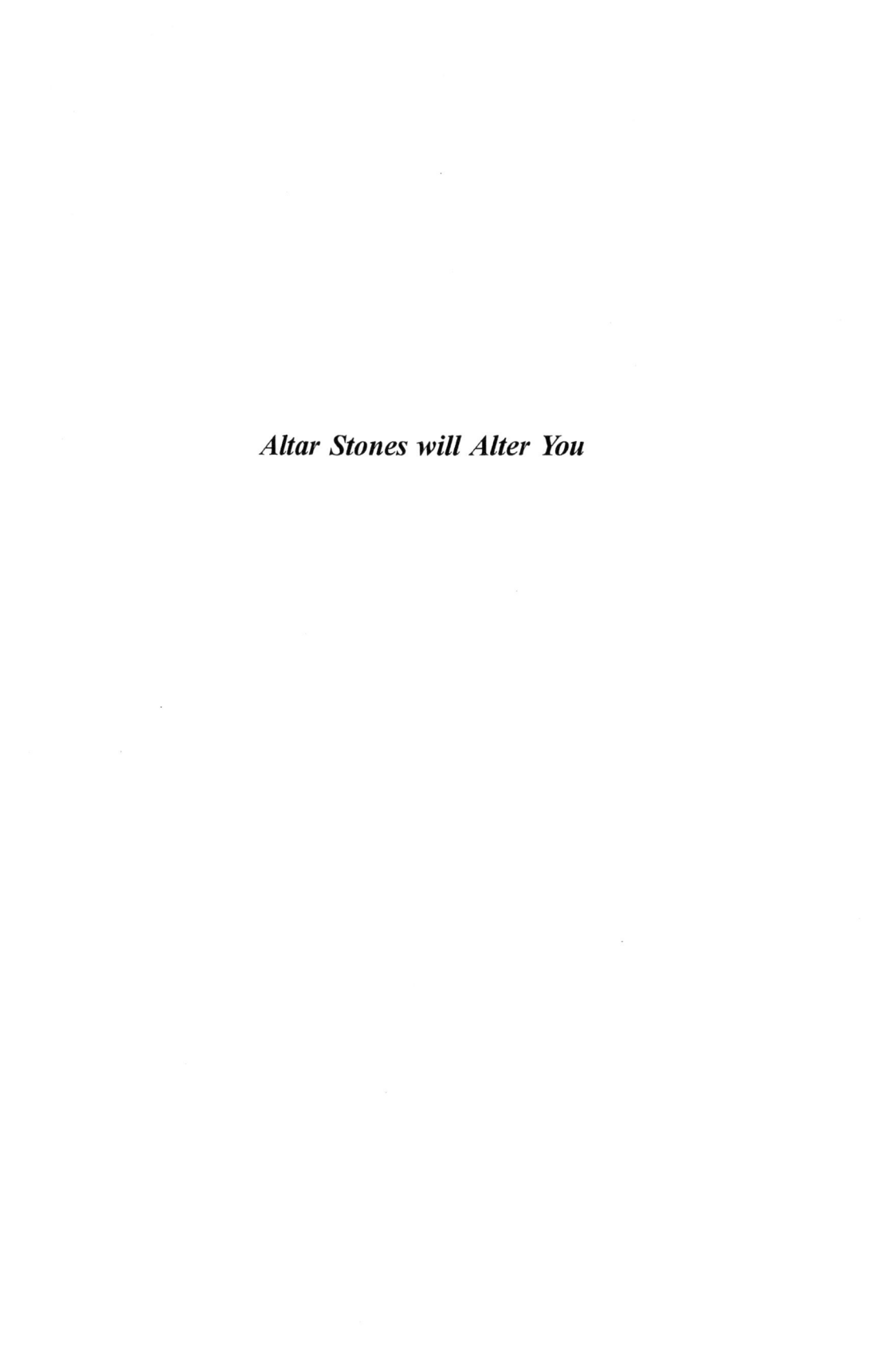

Pilgrims walk reverently on holy ground, hoping to be altered by the place more than it is altered by them. And a consciousness of the omnipresent divine makes any stone into an appropriate altar. Some travelers have been drawn to remote areas of the world intending to search out the wisdom of a place. Others wish simply to find a heightened sense of the site's ability to enlighten. Sometimes a seeker goes to the shrine to experience holiness and takes home an enhanced awareness of the pervasive sacred.

So it is that the seasoned traveler learns what the demanding tourist does not: The way one moves through the world, one's capacity to embrace what is different or difficult, is intimately connected to the way life will be conducted in familiar surroundings. We may find, in each of these poems, a moment of insight, no matter how fleeting. There is likely to be alteration in the very perception of a seeker who has offered at the altar of an ancient sacred space. The singularity of one's own domain, despite its shortcomings, will become one of the treasures the world sends home with the returning traveler.

Carolyne Wright

EULENE BETWEEN ACTS

What now, Eulene? Your eyes blink open
on the dew-slick steps of the holy city,
mist drifting over the river before dawn
like the prehistoric musings of the Aryan gods.
What wisdom do you fathom
in the Ganges' sacred slime?
What knowledge or what power put on
from the garlanded remains of sages
rowed out amidst the mournful chants
of their shaven–headed devotees
and dropped into mid–stream
from yellow cloths block–printed
with the names of God?

Not for you the harrowing of hell,
underwater halls of the afterworld.
Not for you the ash–smeared breast,
sandalpaste streaks on the forehead,
the matted hair and crazed eyes
of the Seer. Not for you the zero
at the center of the Sacred Word.

What goes under must rise again
say the apotheosophists, repeating
the sacrificial hero's thousand names,
giving the ancient story's prayer wheel
one more spin. You, too,
have thrashed your way to the surface,
gasping for air in a language
not your own: its babble all around you
no more meaningless
than the trillion–year–old hum of galaxies
whirling in subatomic space.

>   Except you recall
> that nothing comes of nothing
> and there's nothing of you written
> in the pages of your lost love's book.
>
> Nothing to do but stand up,
> still swaying like marsh grass
> in the oily undulations slapping the steps
> where you first clambered out.
> Then stagger off, up dark medieval lanes
> between cows and refugee vendors' stalls
> and children begging among images
> of the uncreated Lord—toward
> something beyond either praise or blame.
>
> Ready, at last, for anything.

Author's Note: In the sacred city of Varanasi (Banaras), the bank of the Ganges River is lined with ancient Hindu temples. The *ghats*, steps leading down to the river, are used for cremation of dead Hindu faithful, many of whom travel to Varanasi in their last days so as to be able to die in one of Hinduism's most holy places. Although most Hindus practice cremation of their dead, the bodies of some priests and infants are simply wrapped in *namaboli* (cloth printed with prayers) and lowered into the river.

Sandra Olson

THE ROAD TO MUKTINATH

Helicopters cut through
the cool morning air
for those with bank accounts
to rival their devotion.
Others drape their flowing robes
over donkeys, mules and ponies.
But most move themselves—
their prayer wheels and tikas,
backpacks and cameras—
toward the temples of earth,
water and fire.

Some have waited all their lives
and make the quest
on legs old enough
to know what it means.
There are porters and accountants,
grandmothers and monks,
turning away from the world
by climbing toward the clouds
or testing their earthly forms
with aching muscles, straining breath
to prove themselves alive.

A swollen tendon makes me choose
between the journey
and the ankle-gripping, all-protecting boots
that have brought me this far.
Feet vulnerable
without padding, deep tread,
arch support,
I move slowly over broken pebbles
and slippery, boulder-bridged streams,
feeling the shape and texture of the trail,
every rut or sharp edge
I would have missed yesterday.

And I notice all the shoes—
from high tech gortex–insulated, shock–proof
to the lightest, treadless thongs,
a bearded saddhu
with only his callouses.

The peaceful gazes
of those coming toward me
may only be because
they are walking downhill,
but they've been where I'm going
so I greet them with a smile.
A woman in a bright sari
returns the smile
and words I think I understand.
Our feet are covered
by similar sparse layers.
I step into her footprint
as she steps into mine.

Author's Note: Muktinath, in the Himalayas of Nepal, draws pilgrims from all over the world. Trekkers following the Southern Annapurna circuit from Jomosom mingle with Buddhist monks, Hindu holy men, Tibetan traders, and mountaineers descending from the treacherous Thorung La Pass. Inside Jiwali Mayi Mandir, the town's main temple, there is a spring and an eternal flame, uniting the elements of earth, water, and fire.

David Whyte

THE FACES AT BRAGA

In monastery darkness
by the light of one flashlight
the old shrine room waits in silence.

While above the door
we see the terrible figure,
fierce eyes demanding. "Will you step through?"

And the old monk leads us,
bent back nudging blackness
prayer beads in the hand that beckons.

We light the butter lamps
and bow, eyes blinking in the
pungent smoke, look up without a word,

see faces in meditation,
a hundred faces carved above,
eye lines wrinkled in the hand held light.

Such love in solid wood!
Taken from the hillsides and carved in silence
they have the vibrant stillness of those who made them.

Engulfed by the past
they have been neglected, but through
smoke and darkness they are like the flowers

we have seen growing
through the dust of eroded slopes,
their slowly opening faces turned toward the mountain.

Carved in devotion
their eyes have softened through age
and their mouths curve through delight of the carver's hand.

If only our own faces
would allow the invisible carver's hand
to bring the deep grain of love to the surface.

If only we knew
as the carver knew, how the flaws
in the wood led his searching chisel to the very core,

we would smile too
and not need faces immobilized
by fear and the weight of things undone.

When we fight with our failing
we ignore the entrance to the shrine itself
and wrestle with the guardian, fierce figure on the side of good.

And as we fight
our eyes are hooded with grief
and our mouths are dry with pain.

If only we could give ourselves
to the blows of the carver's hands,
the lines in our faces would be the trace lines of rivers

feeding the sea
where voices meet, praising the features
of the mountain and the cloud and the sky.

Our faces would fall away
until we, growing younger toward death
every day, would gather all our flaws in celebration

to merge with them perfectly,
impossibly, wedded to our essence,
full of silence from the carver's hands.

Author's Note: Braga on my first visit, in 1979, was untouched and unvisited. The temple is now but a stone's throw away from the Annapurna circuit.

Jody Bolz

PRAMBANAN, JAVA

In seasons of rain
the jungle widens—
denying borders of black sand,
encompassing volcanoes

with sentient ferns, arch bamboo,
a million fruiting palms.
The rain exhausts itself
on so much growth,

lush without limit,
and the trees let go:
rush to press their masts
against a bright body of cloud.

I've never heard a sound
as sad and as sure,
though this is *my* voice
chanting for Shiva:

a big stone shape
enshrined at Prambanan.
Whoever carved his face
must have been surprised to see

how gracefully, implacably,
it registers each death
and stands accountable—
how smooth the lips and eyelids,

how lovely the look
of all that besets us.

Author's Note: Prambanan is a stunning 10th century Hindu temple near Jogjakarta in East Java. Set among palms in view of volcanoes, the central temple's stone chambers house figures of Hindu deities, including Shiva, the destroyer, whose countenance is androgynously beautiful and harrowing in its impassivity. The curved walls of the individual chambers carry sound in such a way that a single voice can sing in harmony, each note circling back to join the notes that follow.

Glenna Holloway

THE ENLIGHTENED ONE

"Only the lucky awake under skies clear enough to see Mt. Fuji."
—Travel World

Fujiyama: Haunting as haiku,
mine to see only in misty colors on silk scrolls.
Two weeks I waited for audience with its majesty,
hanging rice paper pleas on Japanese cedars,
hiking the Hakone hills to knock on doors
of cumulus, watching red ferries stroke the lake
below. Once, struggling up Fuji's flanks,
I had touched it like truth, held it hugely—
unidentifiable.

Strong Shinto winds urged me to Kamakura.
Still the mountain sat coveting privacy
like an ancient shogun enshrined in smoke
from a billion censers, unmoved by my petitions,
contemplating old crucibles beneath his throne.

As my home flight began, I stared at emptiness
in my gold lacquer memory box, my only keepsake.
Absently I fingered its silk lining as we rose
above the cloud stacks. Then off the starboard wing—
a *bodhisattva*.

Pedestaled on ermine and lapis, Helios–haloed,
caped in white lotus—Bodhisattva Fujiyama.
Electing to stay this side of heaven,
giving a glimpse inside the meaning of light,
forcing shut earthly eyes.

But my gilded box—still much too full to close.

Author's Note: A bodhisattva is a soul who has earned the right to enter Nirvana and eternal peace, but chooses instead to remain on earth to help enlighten others.

Jeffrey Loo

IN KAMAKURA (JAPAN)

The old temple's thatch ceiling
is a blanket two meters thick
blackened by the smoke of a million burning prayers
yet the candles expand the high dark space
shining on the tawny and green–brown grass.
This shrine is where I bury the past.
I light candles for my true and false selves
no longer debating which is which
because delusions need burials too.
Our delusions are everything we are
plus cash, flawless love, fame and perfect wisdom.
They are more than we ever know ourselves to be...
It is raining now and
I want to stay here,
to go up through the grass ceiling,
to leave behind every thing I am, was, or will be.
But this place has lived without me
for a thousand years—
it is an offering in itself,
an act I only dream of,
its life simplified continuously through the clear lens,
the disciplined eye, and the endless work
devotion is.

Author's Note: Kamakura in central Honshu, Japan, has many Buddhist shrines, including a famous 42 foot Buddha from 1252. Since Zen Buddhist art styles did not appear in Japan until the Kamakuri period, 1170-1350 AD, the shrine in the poem could not have been literally 1000 years old, but it was one of the oldest.

Carol Nolde

HORUS' EYE

So many forties' films begin on trains—
The camera focuses on a woman's white legs
crossed beneath a smart suit, maybe
a veil falling from a hat set at an angle
to cover thick–lashed eyes above
a full, dark mouth we know must be red.
Opposite, a man barks words and smoke
between a narrow line of lips—his eyes,
slits from smoke or stealth, take her in.
In truth, I'm hatless in a flowered skirt beside
my husband, who also doesn't look the part,
but here we are skimming across the desert.

The tick of the rails, steady as an old projector
on rewind, takes us past the black and white reel
to ancient times that flicker in the frame of our window,
but the women who kneel on the banks are real.
Not posed in prayer, they bend to the Nile
to dip the clothes they rub against rocks
while a shadoof lifts a bucket for white–robed
men who feed the green they've planted in rows
along the banks. Sometimes a donkey
driven circle after circle turns
a wheel that raises river to field,
Archimedes' modern way to water.

We are headed south against the current
to the Aswan Dam that does not allow
the north flowing Nile to flood its banks,
instead transforms its force to light.
As the train moves forward taking us back
toward the river's source, I stare
at people bent over work
that has not changed though centuries have passed.

Knowing Stones

They only glance at the silver snake that slides
along the rail and at our faces framed in glass.
They do not know that film winds behind
my eyes, records the silent mystery of their lives
so when our plane rises above the desert
brown, I will look down into the muddy river
racing between strips of green and unreel
a past that lies beyond all living memory.

Author's Note: The contrast between ancient customs and modern technology was never more startling than in the views of farm life along the Nile as I traveled from Cairo to Aswan. The train I was on, the dam I headed toward were as removed from the daily lives of the poor as their reality was from me.

Sharon Scholl

OLDUVAI

This is as close
as we can come
to home,

As close as sense
can take us
toward its source,

As close as mind
can bring us to the distant
shores of memory.

In the vast scar
bleeding down through Africa
time tears earth
to bone, to shards
of skull whose blank
sockets stare out bluntly
with a human gaze.

Here among the anthropoid
remains we yearn
to recognize the first green
fistula protruding from the simian
tree, the chromosomal twig
that burst into a branch.

But time has left no trace
of memory, not a flicker
of recall betrays the link.

No faint remembrance
here of ancient earth
stirs in our primal brain:

Only an intuition
that in such broken places
we might find ourselves.

Author's Note: African site of the Leakeys' discoveries tracing early hominid evolution; part of the Great Rift Valley running from the Red Sea down through South Africa. Here is probably the lost core of human origins.

Anthony Russell White

FLOATING OVER KALA–LLIT–NUNAATI

A red balloon drifts by the Lufthansa porthole
at 32,000 feet as Greenland slides by below—
vast white plain marked with tiny parallel lines.

We were a million white pilgrims
assembled with a courageous plan
to march together to some far distant
Inuvialluit holy place, but had each
managed to move only a short distance so far.

Land of white, where cloud is merely the lightest
form of snow–in–motion, and island is the heaviest.

We were a herd of like–minded rocks,
tired of the incessant winds, who voted
to emigrate to the seashore to see
if the rumors of liquid water were true.

A 300–watt moon behind tattered–lampshade clouds
illumines silent *Kala–Llit–Nunaati*.

We were heavy Arctic tumbleweeds, numbers
beyond counting, blown the same exact
direction and distance by one chilling gust,
leaving only the short trail of our adventure behind.

The twin black contrail of Lufthansa flight 454
streams along in silence.

And I am white pilgrim, tired rock, tumbleweed,
plowing through the cold snow of this life,
guarding the glowing hot red spark inside.

The Arctic wind howls around me, and I look up
at the balloon, still rising, swollen in the thin air.

Author's Note: *Kala-Llit-Nunaati* is the name the indigenous peoples of Greenland call their homeland. As I flew over it in clear weather I saw a vast white space marked by unexplained straight lines. In my journal I began to speculate what might have caused those lines.

Rose Rosberg

INGENUE IN BALI

Such a golden light! And yet they carve
monsters above
temple doorways. Under cloudless blue
huge–fanged grins.

Devotees gentle as rippling water place
fruit and flowers
before Kali the Black Goddess as though
death were a bride.

At dusk my nightmares dance in demon masks;
drums, gamelans
high–pitched as panic move me
inside one actor in trance; he stabs himself,
he is impregnable.

Keyed beyond fear, joining the villagers,
I relish terror
like a hot–spiced sauce. The monstrous
ripens me: I divine

why little girls are taught to twist
like snakes slowly uncoiling;
dreamily they weave their sinuous flow
into almost boneless arms. They are learning
how to convert the repulsive into grace.

Author's Note: Bali in Indonesia was a magical island. Much wood carving, especially of deities, is done by local artisans.

Kathy Kennedy Tapp

REFLECTIONS AT NEWGRANGE

Labyrinth tunnel snakes through rock,
winds toward ancient passage tomb.
"A thousand years before Stonehenge"
explains the Irish guide.
Newgrange. Old darkness.
On winter's solstice,
wan morning sun finds
the waiting rock window
and fills cave with gold.

Silent stones mark the entrance.
Spirals etch rocks,
call the sun:
       we believe; we hope.
       Come back.

A pendant.
Spirals carved in white bone,
hangs over my heart,
guards the tomb.
Lines swirl outward—
energy of chambered nautilus,
Van Gogh's sky, Milky Way.
Pale bone summons light. Pleads.
       Prays.
            Find the window.
            Come back.

Author's Note: The megalithic passage-tomb of Newgrange, Ireland, 280 feet in diameter, was built 5000 years ago by Stone Age farmers. Large stone slabs etched with spirals and zigzags surround its base. A 62 foot passageway leads to an internal burial chamber. A slit in the "roof box" above the mound's entrance allows the first rays of winter solstice sun to shine into the chamber.

Kathleen Cain

DAUGHTERS

for Kelly

"The wind has bundled up the clouds high over Knocknarea, and thrown the thunder on the stones for all that Maeve can say."

—W. B. Yeats, *Red Hanrahan's Song About Ireland.*

    A green track through the fields leads to the queen's cairn on Knocknarea—the Hill of the Queen. Queen Maeve. Two men are in the field, father and son. Their faces are like mirrors, like this: when he looks into the fact of his son's eyes, the old one, if he has any sensibility about him at all, and it is plain that he does, sees himself twenty-five years ago. He walked to the top of the hill every day then. Or rode the horse. His hair had not gone streaky grey then, thin as strands of winter sun. His face was not like leather then, tanned with storms and the sea-cold clouds. He could still see a beam of light in the waves.

    He salutes us. The red-haired son says nothing, smiles like a fox. Their blue tractor moves slower than we do. Two daughters. Returned Americans. Facing into the hill. Looking for Maeve. Looking for Yeats. Looking for Red Hanrahan. Looking for some part of ourselves that might have been dropped by the side of the road, like a stone or a brick of turf.

    The men are replacing fenceposts. The weather rots them quickly until falling and rotting become a motion all of one kind. Carved to a point and tarred for the ground, one timber slides off the tractor. Then another. Still one more. I side-step, but do not break my stride in bending to the task. My sister doesn't either.

    The old one dismounts. Laughing. No teeth left in his mouth but two. Embarrassed, but not surprised. These are daughters. And daughters expect to help.

Author's Note: The cairn atop Knock na Rea, the "Hill of the Queen", near Sligo, Ireland, can be seen from many miles away. Legend has it that the remains of Medbh (Maeve), the warrior queen of Connaught, rest there.

Richard Fammerée

ASLEEP IN IRELAND

My forehead touches folds and stone. It is mud
and gold. It is sky
silvered. Its curls fondle a puddle where fingers abandon
the wind to huddle as babies
at my breast.

I am asleep in a weaving field in Sligo, and the earth
mothers me.
Oh, how I love my sleep in Ireland.

All that has transpired during the previous nine years
is now a dream. When I awake
to myself unblemished, dressed again in juniper:
I did not invite Deborah to Dublin.
We were not married in the Shelbourne Hotel.
We did not abandon the family in Wicklow,
and the family in Wicklow did not abandon me.
I did not retreat with her to Germany.
There was no divorce one year later.
I did not soil my story, and my story did not soil me.
I did not lose my adventure.

I first knelt in this dimple of nettles and puddles upon
the forty-second day of my great pilgrimage.

The sun was my shield, the fields unlettered and not dying.
I lay my bag next to this rock and lay my head
upon my bag.

I slept to the rhythm of cows
and clouds, the moon, invisible in cerulean, wandering
and blessing the shore of me
asleep upon this belly, burning with the yolks of furze
flowering into the big, dreamy, beating silence
of the embryo.

Hobo licks my palm. We walk hills wet, wax
green and valleys wetter and greener.
The sheep farmers do not concern him.
They have not yet poisoned him. He is turning away
and turning back, orange and lime in the sun.

He is an Alsatian like me and a stray. When he died, I
buttoned him into my flannel shirt and buried him beneath
a plum tree.

We sleep now in Ireland, separated only by the vast mirror
of earth. I bite into fruit nourished by his body.
Hobo knows me as I enter the mulberry trees.
My mother greets us from an iron chair. She rises. She, too,
is smiling victoriously. She is lantern lit, beautiful again.
I knew that she could beat the cancer.
I knew that she was still alive. I say to her,
*Now, don't be upset. But there was a time I didn't know
you. Years and years when you wore your hair like this–*
[I gesture.] *All lost. All that time is lost.*
She begins to cry, but we are together again.
Before I can introduce Hobo, I awake.

I begin to move my limbs.
There is gray in my beard but I cannot see it, for I have
no mirror. I believe that I am healed.

I believe that I am healed. All that I have dreamed is real.
All that has shortened my breath and scarred me
is a dream.

With what god do I negotiate this arrangement?
And what more must I offer?

Author's Note: Troubadouring across Europe, I fell from a half–eaten apple into dreams in the very place I had rested and dreamt a decade before. I trembled with the thrill of superstition, but have since learned that there are no coincidences.

Kathleen Cain

ALL THAT YOU NEED, SHE SAYS: A DREAM OF POUL NA BRONE DOLMEN

Suddenly she's in the field on foot.
No car, no donkey, the way a dream
transports the dreamer. Dolmen house,
all that's left of some poor Celt's
mounded grave inhabited again.

Dream on a warrior's grave
and the doors to the Otherworld
will open to you.

A cloth of pattern and weave
she does not know
curtains the passage, makes
an ancient song in the wind,
coins on its edges
older than any Caesar forged, even before
sunlight gleaming on the Rubicon
hurt his eyes. The wind rattles stones
along the Burren, shakes the bushes
to their roots. She passes the veil
in darkness, finds an old woman within.

Hidden Ireland, forced to conceal herself
in Iron Age tombs among the hills,
to reveal herself
to her children's
children's
children's
children's
immigrant
child.

Only her eyes, like blue discs
or smoke in the distance, give her away.
She offers a gift. A palm full of stones.
A part of herself. She has not learned
to make rosaries yet.

The white one
for clarity and light. Make anger
to burn away darkness from it, she says,
but the darkness is also a gift.

The black one,
the largest, takes
longer to gather, less light
to dispel. Dream it.

The brown one for
the things of earth, its
bottom always tinged with blood,
the hunt, birth. The earth
dies in order to live.
Walk inside the circle. Keep it.

Red for Love, the heart, one edge
scoured with disappointment, the rest
growing open, ready to receive.

Grey-green, a wedge of the sea,
of the air that hangs above the sea,
of clouds the sea gives birth to,
what you cannot see through yourself,
the grey-green places that fill a life.

Begin again.
Use your clarity now.
Burn fog, fear, dry leaves, old love, untruth
away. Use all that you need. Five strengths
from myself to yourself
in the palm of your hand, she says.

Author's Note: Poul na Brone Dolmen, with its two upright walls and its angled roof of stone, is all that remains of an ancient burial site in an area in County Clare, Ireland known as the Burren which resembles nothing so much as the mountains of the Moon.

Madeleine Beckman

NOTTINGHAM

Years ago, digging–up ancient civilizations
I glimpsed myself in a flash of trowel
side by side with the delicate skull of a woman
thousands of years old. I was with her
in the summer heat.
Wild lavender saturated the air,
blonde wheat–fields, shoulder–high
fused into birds, butterflies,
sounds of countryside, sounds
Turner, Chaucer, Arthur heard.

Years ago, digging up ancient civilizations
I dug for myself, looking for where I lay
hidden, beneath mounds of earth,
but safe,   safe
beneath blue sky
in a farmer's field
far enough away
from the teeth of the plow, yet
fortunate finally to be found.

Author's Note: Nottingham, in England's north country, is Robin Hood's domain. Eating meat pies, drinking ale and singing at the local tavern fills one's day. Here a thick mystical mist lingers over the rolling countryside. In this close knit community of row houses, in an ashen residue from decades of mining, are echoes of millennia past.

Deanne Bayer

GRANADA

Seared by the breath
of desert wind
from across the Mediterranean,
I chase relief in shadow, wilt
through streets ribboned
by Holy Day celebrants
and haunted by spirits of Moors
parading beside plaster saints
flamboyant in sequins, satin, gilt.

No weeds grow at the side
of the path, choked
with the taste of dust. Below,
Granada crouches
in the mountain's palm. Climbing
to the Alhambra
under the demon sun, I pass
crumbled towers,
once a sultan's sentinels,
to reach courtyard gardens misted
by a fountain of steps
and filigree stonework
transcending time and defeat.

Within the great hall's
roofed shade, my fingers inhale
cool tiles
still blazoning their colors
as though the Arab artisans
who baked this beauty
will return any moment
to fire the kiln, as though
unfaded opulence
can nullify heat and thirst
and history. Missiles of light

Knowing Stones

invade through an arch
framing a hillside vista
vanquished now by scrub
and rock, where native Spaniards
once secluded in caves
while the Moors
indulged appetites
for building palaces
and brought their numinous math to Iberia.

I have come from a world
stridently demolishing yesterday
to find comfort
where past centuries
coated with time's slow flow
dig their heels
into the mountain, refusing the cup.

Author's Note: Influences of Moorish architecture and art permeate this region of Spain, which once shone with the light of Moorish civilization while Europe was still in the Dark Ages.

Tom Roby

PRESSURE POINTS

Malta's Grand Harbour, faceless fortress,
obdurate against Saracen and Nazi,
compels respect because
it also guards the
world's oldest
temples.

But what meanings are in these beginnings:
what use their cloverleaf emblems;
why lunar mother has no head,
or two; whose blood flowed
over thick skirted legs
beneath her torso
altar and was
bleached
away?

Such lore is not bought from tour guides.
Lost priests, forgotten gods
left us to find answers
from earth and sky
by our rituals,
unaided.

At Hagar Qim, stone bones of carved devotion
lack the muscles to move me. Twined
with spiraling spirits of sacred
vines, pock patterned as a
thousand peacocks' eyes,
they are blinder
than Tiresias
and less
vocal.

I fill blank sockets with ten finger tips,
hope right pressure hallows space,
for new moons to fix fickle
faith. Slowly, I pull
back my tingling
fingers until I
lose touch.

Knowing Stones

The silent ferryman weighs my
anchor of questions. Blood
sun sinks into water. Its
crust stains Homer's
sea wine dark. I
turn away to
a secular
supper.

Author's Note. Sixty miles south of Sicily lies Malta with its grand harbor whose wonderful geometry was built of stone after the Great Siege of 1565 in which the Knights of St. John beat off Suleiman's Turks. At Hagar Qim (meaning "standing stones") are temples that date back five millenia. Archaeologists refer to the pocked stones unpoetically as "pitted megaliths."

Joseph Powell

EASTER IN AEGINA

Beneath the shattered Temple of Apollo,
a sky bluer than the Limbourg's May,
my son splashes naked into the surf,
glistening with salt and sunlight.
His soft unblemished body is beautiful.

Beauty, music, light, the body's truth:
what god can hold them up to soothe
the crucifixions of the spirit,
its body's modesties?

When a sweet corruption rankles
I see, not five steps away,
a dog, dead and sinking into sand.
He's the sea's castaway.
The rusted collar that dragged him down
still rings his neck, studded with rust.
Flies mumble, ants trickle back and forth.
The beach is littered with plastic and paper.

All the gods are dying.
Bored with eternity, themselves,
they're homesick for our attention:
the sculptor's hands that drew
Apollo out of the olive wood,
felt the smoothness of his cheek,
shaped the temple vein, his muscled ribs,
chiseled out the quaint curves
of his genitals, the arched toes, his lips.

Knowing Stones

From some stubborn height,
my Christian soul looks down at me:
the sea, my son in the surf,
blue light like dolphins leaping.

Aesop's fat well–dressed dog is corrupt,
and that mangy cautious wolf
ranges pine forests of the mind.

I feel the dog's dilemma,
the collar's itch and heat,
that wolf–instant that made him jump
unleashed into the sea.

Author's Note: Aegina, a Saronic island a short boat ride from the port of Pireaus, can be seen from the Acropolis in Athens. The Temple of Apollo, with only one broken column still standing, is on the outskirts of the island's major town, Aghia Marina.

B. A. St. Andrews

AZTECS

You stand in sacred Aztec dirt
staring at temples but alert
to one fact only: your

feet hurt. Those broken ruins
rise toward the same relentless
sun which has nearly gouged

your eyes. Your head pounds;
your Madras skirt winds
like red tape round and around

your ever modest thighs. With fervor
you decide those slick brochures
back home have a great deal to

atone for. They pictured none of this
yet led you here to wonder, in
pinched surprise, if you're the tourist

or the sacrifice. You find a bench.
The guide is speaking now in tongues
(Spanish, German, French)

and suddenly you sense
time opening its secret door
that slides you to the past.

Your breath comes fast.
You stand alone inside a ring
of broken stone aghast to hear

(whorling against your inner ear)
the astonished victim's
cry. He is trembling nearby.

Knowing Stones

Caught up is some invisible
procession, you climb (one by
one) the hundred fourteen steps

to the Altar of Sacrifice. With
a flash the obsidian knife
lifts and cuts your heart in half.

You bury earthly desire and fall
into the purifying fire. Then,
as suddenly, all is still. When

you can, you will again climb down
to take your place upon that
rusted bus to town. Car phones,

sirens, tepid tonics laced with
lime will slap you back to
time. One guide will understand

and, taking you aside, will slide
a holy fragment of temple stone
inside your fisted hand.

Author's Note: In Tenochtitlán, on the site of present day Mexico City, great stone temples were terraced pyramids called *teocalli* at the top of which stood a flat stone of sacrifice. This poem celebrates the human connections that transcend time and culture, revelations that often come with physical discomfort or exhaustion of travel when, defenses down, metaphysical reality opens within and around us like a hidden door.

Jonathan Harrington

RUINS

A man,
camera strung around his neck,
his shirt, shorts and sandals
bought this morning
in the native market,
stands atop a pyramid
surveying the ruins
of an ancient city.
A mound of stones to the east,
a frescoed temple to the north,
the stalls of the deserted market
forever open to the jungle.
Iguanas, scurrying to hidden places,
scrape their scaly hides
on the cracks
between granite blocks.
Below, in the temple
the man's wife is running
her hands along the carvings,
feeling the lips
of the imperial governor
and the shoulder
of his warrior.
This could be the couple's
last vacation together. Perhaps
each one is thinking, but not believing,
how everything could come to ruin
in a second.
Why did they come so innocently
to this ruined city?
Were they thinking that somewhere
among the rubble and broken gods
was some lost part of themselves
that they hoped to find?

Author's Note: This poem, set in the Yucatan Peninsula of Mexico, questions why we travel, and more specifically, why people are attracted to ruined cities.

John Gilgun

MAYAN PYRAMID, YUCATAN PENINSULA

The sun, having no say in the matter, plunges
into the jungle
Heartbeat retreats backward into heartbeat
Breath retreats backward into breath
Silence retreats backward into silence
Black hole retreats backward into black hole
black water into black water, *cenote* into *cenote*

You must become chaos

The sun, having no alternative, plummets into the jungle
The blossom retreats backwards into the bud
The eye of the scribe retreats backwards into the glyph
You are retreating into the small soil of your bones
As the bird retreats into its cry
As the jungle retreats into its shadow
As the ants, in their long corridors of Dreamlight
retreat backwards into the sun
The sun, having no choice, vanishes into the jungle
You, having no choice, vanish into the limestone of your bones

You must be born again as chaos

A jaguar is retreating backwards into the Underworld
into Xibalba, the sun in his jaws, the sun
in his teeth, the sun in his throat, the sun
in his belly, the sun in his ears, the sun
in his balls, the sun in his paws, the sun
in his claws, the sun in his cock, the sun
in his eyes, the sun in his blood, the sun
in his heart, the sun in his sperm

You must be born again through this
This sacrificial bliss   This

Author's Note: At a conference in Quintana Roo, near the border with Belize, we were taken by bus to a pyramid of secret location not yet fully excavated. An archaeologist told us this legend: the jaguar god captures the sun in its teeth at sunset and carries it through the terrifying depths of the Underworld, emerging at sunrise to another day of light.

Richard Beban

FOR MY BEST FRIEND, WHO HAS SEEN MIRACLES

You, who trod the pilgrim's labyrinth
at Chartres, circled the thousand–domed temple
of Shiva at Prambanan in Java,
wrote poems in the shadow of
Sultan Ahmet's Blue Mosque at dusk,
come to me with a tale of a miracle
surpassing these.

How your eyes flame,
your face grows soft with wonder,
you describe circumscribing *this* miracle
first in anger & fear, then melting
into tenderness,
finally an endless *frisson* of awe.

You tell me how she lays
her hand soft upon the *stupa* of her belly,
so protective when she sleeps or
in distracted moments during the day.

How love arrives in surges & you barely have time
for a breath before your head is under water again.
Finally, you succumb and surprise! you can breathe
this weightier stuff, live in this medium, too,
travel between the realms with equal grace.

I have never seen your face like this
not at Giverney in Monet's springtime garden,
at Joyce's home in Dublin,
in our treks through Paris cafes or the
fevered, four–in–the–morning streets
of Marseilles.

Knowing Stones

They have a machine, you say,
that lets you see him yourself,
translucent fingers,
his nose already the shape of yours,
even the testicles & tiny bud
of his penis. Radar picture on a cathode tube
—see his tiny heart flutter
faster than a hummingbird. How he quickens
inside her whose hand you hold in this sterile room
that beats with life.

You & I who have suffered fathers
& loved them nonetheless
have feared this journey.
But you act now as a man acts
in the face of something greater.
It is beyond your control, you say,
demeanor is all that counts,
doing the inevitable well.

Our fathers never saw us deep inside
our mother's bellies, never saw us take shape
the way you can see your son, before the wounds
of birth & growth & those you will inflict
with tongue & hand. He sleeps in that perfect
sac of bliss & water storing up love for you
the way we loved our fathers, despite their mistakes
—two of which
might have been us.

As you have taught me before,
when we traveled, you teach me again, pilgrim.
The lesson this time:
How deep awe rests at the center
of the word father.

Author's Note: For Phil Cousineau, with whom I have traveled to many exotic places. Still, the greatest joy of our friendship has been watching him travel through the realm of fatherhood. A stupa (Sanskrit for "mound") is a Buddhist monument of mound–like shape.

Jonathan Harrington
TREASURES

Inside of you,
out of the weather
and the corruption of silverfish,
you carry your treasures:
the glances of lovers
collected in parks under moonlight
beneath leafless trees,
and rivers;
their sources, your heart,
their mouths, yours.
The shouts of children
in a hundred languages
echo inside your trunk.
You carry the wounds
of an army of soldiers
each of a different flag
and the deaths of all the corpses
they struggled to pile on one another.
Inside you there is a vast ocean
and a vast desert
where only one blade of grass grows.
Trains run on their single–minded tracks
over mountains
and the lost lie sleeping in ditches
beside temples of god.
Roads run in every direction
to every city in the world
and flying machines
rise in your chest and sunken vessels
rust in your blood.
Your being is a vault
that is never locked
and therefore keeps filling.
Outside there is nothing
you can put your hands on
but a worn suit of cotton
and a pair of leather sandals.
Inside, the planets rotate
and the stars flicker like tongues of fire.
The sun rises in your eyes
and sets in your well–worn feet.

Author's Note: Traveling provides a wonderful exposure to the world outside. But the treasures of the world are to be found within each and every one of us.

Contributors

M. Eliza Hamilton Abegunde served for two months with Captain Bill Pinkney as the lead team teacher for a group of staff and crew retracing by boat part of the route used by slave traders to bring Africans to the Caribbean and South America. She uses poetry and journaling to help students explore and reclaim their cultural histories through movement and various languages. She has won recognition for her continued work to help people understand the impact of the Middle Passage on African descendants and the world.

Lynore Banchoff is a writer and social worker in Rhode Island, where she has a clinical practice and does education and support on the Internet. She was born in California and has lived in Holland and France. Her poems have appeared in *Friends Journal, Juggler's World, Newport Review,* and the anthologies: *Women and Death* and *Eating Our Hearts Out.*

Steve Barfield lives in North Palm Beach, Florida and works as a literature researcher in medicine. For twenty years he has been a member of the Immanentist School of poetry founded by Duane Locke. Although widely traveled, he has been to Spain and Egypt only in his imagination.

Walter Bargen has published seven books of poems. The latest is *Water Breathing Air* from Timberline Press, 1999. He is the recipient of a National Endowment for the Arts writing fellowship (1991), winner of the Quarter After Eight Prose Prize (1996) and the Chester H. Jones Foundation Poetry Prize (1997).

Michele Battiste visited Prague in July, 1998 to study at the Prague Summer Seminars, a program offered by the University of New Orleans at Charles University. She writes and dances in Albany, New York, and her work has or will soon appear in *So to Speak, Poetry Motel, SoulSpeak, Natural Bridge, ante up* and *Rising to the Dawn: A Rape Survivor's Journey into Healing.*

Richard Beban, a resident of Venice, California, has written poetry since 1993. His poems have appeared in more than thirty small press journals and eleven national anthologies. He and his wife, novelist Kaaren Kitchell, are collaborating on a non-fiction book and a workshop series called "Living Mythically" about incorporating myth into your everyday life.

Madeleine Beckman is a poet, fiction writer, and journalist. She is the author of *Dead Boyfriends* (Linear Arts Books, 1998) which is a poetry collection. Her awards include a New York Foundation for the Arts grant for fiction and a Mary Carolyn Davies Memorial Award from the Poetry Society of America. "Nottingham," was inspired by her stay in northern England while on an archaeological excavation.

Shelley Berc is a novelist and playwright. She has written *The Shape of Wilderness*, (Coffee House Press, 1995), and has just completed a new novel called *Light and Its Shadow* that spans the twentieth century in America. She spent a year traveling in the Andes Mountains of South America studying the descendants of the Incas who continue to live along the ancient Inca Road.

Bruce Berger has completed a prose trilogy about nature and culture in the desert. The first book, *The Telling Distance*, won the 1990 Western States Book Award. Baja California Sur is the subject of *Almost an Island* (University of Arizona Press, 1998). His poems have appeared in *Poetry, Commonweal,* and *Barrons's* and have been collected in *Facing the Music,* (Confluence Press, 1995).

Margaret Blaker has worked in museum labs and archives and is studying Maya archaeology at the University of Central Florida in Orlando. Her poems have appeared recently in *Troubador, The Florida Review,* and *The Dan River Anthology, 2000.* Her verse has appeared in *Amelia, Light Year,* and *The Norton Book of Light Verse.*

Jody Bolz teaches creative writing at George Washington University. Her poetry has appeared recently in such publications as *Ploughshares, Indiana Review, River Styx, The Women's Review of Books, Gargoyle,* and *Poet Lore,* and in a number of anthologies, including *Her Face in the Mirror* (Beacon, 1994). Her book-length poem *False Summit* revisits scenes from a year she spent travelling in Asia, living for several months in both Nepal and Indonesia.

W. K. Buckley received his Ph.D. from Miami University in Oxford, Ohio and currently teaches at Indiana University (Northwest). He has lived in Mexico, England, New York, Kentucky, and Arizona. He has edited and authored several books of literary criticism and published widely in poetry journals. He reads his poetry in Chicago, and sings in Irish pubs the ballads he writes about Druid ruins. His chapbook, *By The Horses Before The Rains* was named 1997's "Best Chapbook of the Year" by *Modern Poetry,* and his work has been nominated for a Pushcart Prize. His book *81 Mygrations* was published in 1998.

Deborah Byrne has lived in the Middle East and Europe, and her travels have taken her throughout Africa, Arabia, southeast and southwest Asia. Both her international photography and her poetry have won awards. Currently she lives in Massachusetts with her cat Emily D. and works at the William Joiner Center for the Study of War and Social Consequences. Everyone there is trying to find her a husband, preferably one who can cook rice and beans. Her poetry has been published in such journals as *The Paterson Literary Review, Crab*

Creek Review, and *The Cimarron Review.*

Kathleen Cain has lived in Ireland and traveled there extensively. She has read her poetry on Irish radio (RTE). Her poems have appeared in several magazines and anthologies, including *Irish Poetry Now: Other Voices.*

Lynda Calabrese has been published in many journals and anthologized in *Filtered Images: Women Remembering Their Grandmothers,* and NC Poetry Society's *Here's to the Land.* Her play, *Dodo's Introduction to the End,* was a winner in Charlotte's Children's Theatre's New Works For Kids contest. Her chapbook, *On the Cusp of Something Else* was published in 1994. She is enriched by her many travels with her husband and two grown children.

Linda Casebeer lives in Birmingham, Alabama and works in medical education for the University of Alabama School of Medicine where she has had the privilege of working with others to develop courses for physicians in Peru. She has recently published poems in various journals including *Slant, Hawaii Pacific Review, Pinyon Poetry,* and the anthology, *The Practice of Peace.*

Kelly Cherry has published five books and three chapbooks of poetry, six books and one chapbook of fiction, one book and one chapbook of essays, and an autobiography entitled *The Exiled Heart* (Louisiana State University Press), which recounts the story of her relationship with the Latvian composer, Imants Kalnin.

Anna Citrino is a native Californian who has been working overseas as a teacher since 1991, currently in Singapore, but previously in Kuwait and Turkey. She is a graduate of the Bread Loaf School of English. Her work has appeared in various literary journals including *Flyway, Kalliope,* and *Bellowing Ark.*

Maureen Micus Crisick teaches literature at the University of Phoenix, Northern California Campus. Her collection of poems, *Night Train to Budapest* was published by Middle Tennessee State University. Her work has appeared in *The American Scholar, Poetry,* and *The Sun,* and was nominated for a 1997 Pushcart Prize. Maureen received a fellowship at Hawthornden Castle International Retreat for Writers in Scotland.

Christopher Conlon travelled extensively in Southern Africa during his stint as a Peace Corps Volunteer in Botswana. His work has appeared in *America, Interrace, The Long Story, Pembroke Magazine,* and numerous other publications.

John Dickson spent many years on the Chicago Board of Trade and operated a grain elevator. He wrote short stories which kept getting shorter and more rhythmic until he realized they were poems. In 1980, when his first book of poetry, *Victoria Hotel*, received a Friends of Literature award, he left the grain business to concentrate on his writing. His next books were *Waving At Trains* and *The Music of Solid Objects*. John has published widely and has received a National Endowment for the Arts grant for poetry.

James Doyle lived in Mexico for a year and visited the Well of Sacrifice on the Yucatan Peninsula. His poems have appeared in two book collections and in over 200 literary journals, including *Poetry, Carolina Quarterly,* and *The Literary Review*. His poetry has been included in such anthologies as *Literature: An Introduction to Critical Reading* (Prentice Hall, 1996).

Karen Douglass lives in Maine, where she works as a healthcare consultant and psychiatric nurse. She has published in many journals and has two books, *Red Goddess Poems* and *Bones in the Chimney*. Currently she is at work on a creative non-fiction book about horses.

Alan Elyshevitz holds an MFA in writing from Bennington College. He has recently had work published in *Alligator Juniper, Half Tones To Jubilee* and *The Baltimore Review*. His poetry chapbook, *The Splinter in Passion's Paw*, was published by New Spirit Press.

Tyler Enfield has been traveling for the last five years, sojourning here and there just long enough to start a few gardens, a family, and a poem or two.

Diane Engle is an attorney, musician, and poet by profession. She has also published articles on adoption and education in newspapers and magazines, and was included in the anthology, *The Muse Strikes Back*. Her poetry has appeared in numerous literary journals in the US and England.

Andrew Epstein's poems and essays have appeared or are forthcoming in *North American Review, Notre Dame Review, Verse, Raritan, Review of Contemporary Fiction*, and *Brooklyn Review*. He is currently completing his Ph.D. in English at Columbia University, where he has been teaching American literature and composition for several years. He is working on a study of friendship and individualism in twentieth-century American poetry.

Richard Fammerée appears in *Who's Who in America* as a poet, composer and performing artist. He is featured in American and European publications and venues, has appeared on National Public Radio, and hosts the radio program Poetry & Its Music International at the University of Chicago. *Lessons of Water and Thirst*, a collection of his poems published by Collage Press, chronicles the spontaneous education of this troubadour who first performed his poetry and played the varnish off a guitar in the Latin Quarter of Paris.

Sandy Feinstein wrote these poems while on a Fulbright Award to Syria during the 1998-99 academic year. She taught at Aleppo University as a senior lecturer/researcher. Presently she administers the Honors Program at Penn State Berks/Lehigh Valley. She has published poetry most recently in *Crab Creek Review*, *XCP*, *Columbia Poetry Review*, and *DisClosure*, among others.

Rina Ferrarelli came from Italy at the age of fifteen. She has taught at the University of Pittsburgh and is now writing and translating full time. Her most recent book publications are *Home is a Foreign Country* (Eadmer Press, 1997), a collection of poetry, and *I Saw the Muses* (Guernica Editions, 1997), a translation of Leonardo Sinisgalli's lyric poems.

Claire T. Feild, is a college English teacher at SUS Community College in Alabama. She has three collections of poems set in the Mississippi Delta in the 1950s. Her most recent poetry acceptances include such journals as *Sophie's Wind*, *The Eclectic Woman*, *Metaphors*, *Indigenous Fiction*, *Crone Chronicles*, *DAYbreak*, *Bloodstone*, *Architrave*, *Neovictorian/Cochlea*, and *Noccalula*. She saw taro fields for the first time in Princeville, Kauai.

Do Gentry has had poems published in *Confluence*, *Sulphur River Literary Review*, *Fourteen Hills*, *Talking River Review*, among others. She received an honorable mention in the 1998 *Icarus* poetry competition. "Sand " is part of a sequence of poems which she wrote after visiting Calanais in the Outer Hebrides of Scotland.

Phillis Gershator's publications include children's books, most recently *Tiny and Bigman*, an adult reference book, and poetry in such anthologies and journals as *Home Planet News*, *Confrontation*, and *The Caribbean Writer*.

Steven Gibson is the author of *Rorscharch Art*, a volume of poetry which has been a finalist in several national competitions. In 1995 he received a writing fellowship from the state of Florida. He is married with two children and teaches at Palm Beach Community College. His poems have appeared in *Poetry*, *Paris Review*, and *New England Review*, among others.

Michael J. Gill, after having lived in Ohio, Wales, Washington State, and Washington DC, went to Ecuador for the language and the landscape. He had been to school, brought home the degrees, labored at construction sites and behind a desk in the tired halls of the federal government. It was time. His chapbooks include *The Atheist at Prayer*, *388 Lines for My Imaginary Goddess*, and *The Solution to the Crisis is Revolution: Graffiti of Ecuador, collected and translated*. His poems have been published widely.

John Gilgun, is a retired teacher of creative writing at Missouri Western College in Saint Joseph, Missouri. As part of his professional obligations, he was required to attend writers' conferences. Two of the poems featured here were written after attending conferences, one at Galway University organized by Billy Collins, and the other in Mexico organized by Trevor Top.

Netta Gillespie begins all travels from Urbana, Illinois, which some might find exotic. She has published poems, essays, and stories, most recently in *Spoon River Poetry Review, Snowbound,* and *Karamu*. Netta is a recipient of an Illinois Arts Council Award for Poetry.

Gary Mex Glazner spent 1998 traveling the world and meeting poets. His travel stories and poems have resulted in the manuscript *Ramblings*. At the inaugural Poetry Olympics held in Stockholm in October, 1998 Glazner placed first in the individual series. His winning poem was "The Oracle of Delphi."

Sandra Goldsmith began writing poetry as a returning adult student. Since then, her poems have appeared in numerous magazines around the country. She currently teaches in the English Department of Purdue University. A Chicago resident, she comes across poetry in skyline views along Lake Michigan and in pedestrians vying with construction sites for a square of space. She seeks to identify such contrasts in her visits to other parts of the world.

Kate Gray lives in Portland, Oregon, teaches at a community college, and travels as much as possible. She earned her MFA from the University of Washington in 1990. She has travelled to Europe, Canada, Mexico, Indonesia, and China, and hopes to dangle her toes in all the world's oceans.

Dan Green is a confirmed traveler, poet and celebrant of life's and the world's surprises. In WWII he was stationed in India and flew 35 missions into China as an air intelligence officer. After the war, he made a career of social work and became executive director of the Red Cross in New York. At ninety-three he is searching out and writing about the few places on the globe he has not seen. Having taken up the study of poetry at eighty-two, he has four collections in print and has published 1600 poems in 350 journals.

William Greenway, Professor of English at Youngstown State University in Ohio, claims Wales as the powerful home of his ancestors, both biological—his Methodist minister grandfather—and literary: Dylan Thomas. He lived there for a year, writing his poetry volume *Simmer Dim,* the Scottish name for "summer dusk," a pagan celebration of the longest day of the year, June 21st, when it never gets darker than twilight.

Jonathan Harrington, when he graduated from the University of Iowa Writers' Workshop, moved to Merida on Mexico's Yucatan Penninsula. Surrounded by Maya ruins, Spanish Colonial architecture, caves, and beaches, he spent an unforgettable year writing poems and a nonfiction book on the Maya of the area. He has published one chapbook: *Handcuffed to the Juke-*

box; edited an anthology of short stories: *New Visions: Fiction by Florida Writers;* authored a collection of essays: *Tropical Son;* and published three mystery novels, *The Death of Cousin Rose, The Second Sorrowful Mystery,* and *A Great Day For Dying.* He now lives and writes in New York City.

Ashley Mace Havird is a free-lance writer whose poems and short stories have appeared in numerous journals and university quarterlies, including the *Virginia Quarterly Review* and *The Texas Review.* Her interest in Crete began in childhood when she read books on archaeology and Greek mythology. She explored the island for several weeks in 1991 and 1994. A resident of Shreveport, Louisiana, Ms. Havird is presently at work on a novel.

Glenna Holloway, a native of Tennessee, is an artist specializing in pastels, enameling, silversmithing and lapidary. The Orient influenced her work long before her first visits. She was the founding president of the Illinois State Poetry Society, and is a six-time winner of "Best of the Best," in Chicago's Poets and Patrons contest. Her poems have appeared in more than a hundred publications, including *Western Humanities Review, Georgia Review, The Formalist, Spoon River Poetry Review, Southern Poetry Review,* and *Saturday Evening Post.* She is the recipient of a 2000 Pushcart Prize.

Kathleen Iddings' fifth poetry book, *Rings of Saturn,* published by West Anglia in 1999, received the publisher's "Decade of Excellence Award". She has received a National Endowment for the Arts fellowship, among many poetry awards. Kathleen has had more than 400 poems published, and is herself Editor/Publisher of La Jolla Poet's Press and San Diego Poet's Press.

Carol Kanter is a psychotherapist in private practice. Her first published poem appeared in *Iowa Woman* in 1995. *Atlanta Review* gave her a 1998 International Merit Award. Her book, *And Baby Makes Three,* (Winston Press, 1983) explores the emotional transition to parenthood. She and her husband live in Evanston, Illinois and are the parents of two daughters.

Pearl Karrer, having earned a degree in microbiology which led to cancer research in Palo Alto, California, now teaches piano, exhibits prints and drawings in juried shows, and writes poetry, often with images of art. Her poems appear in journals and anthologies. "Printmaking" stems from a six week family odyssey in Greece.

Ruth Moon Kempher has "retired" after twenty-one years of teaching at St. Johns River Community College in St. Augustine, Florida. She runs Kings Estate Press. With twenty books of poetry and short prose already published, Ms. Kempher is struggling toward more time for travel and writing. She has been to many of the world's exotic places.

Claire Keyes, in her travels to Ireland, the birthplace of her parents, has found both the familiar and the exotic in the land and its amazing people. Her poems have appeared most recently in *The Onset Review, Spoon River Poetry Review,* and *Kimera. Rising and Falling* won the Foothills Poetry Chapbook competition in 1999. She lives in Marblehead, Massachusetts.

Katie Kingston teaches Spanish, English, and poetry at Trinidad State College in Colorado, and continues to travel to Mexico twice a year to visit the various ruins and archaeological sites. She has published widely in anthologies and literary magazines and continues to find inspiration for her poetry in the diverse landscape and history of Mexico.

John Knoepfle has taught for many years in the greater St. Louis area. He is now retired from Sangamon State University. His first book of poems was "Rivers into Islands." He won the Mark Twain award for contributions to midwestern literature for his book "Poems from the Sangamon." He was the 1986 Illinois State Author of the Year, and the first recipient of the Illinois Center for the Book Award. He has four children and travels in Ireland to explore his heritage.

Jacqueline Kudler teaches writing and literature at the College of Marin in Kentfield, California. An avid traveler, she and her husband realized a long cherished fantasy—a month long safari through Kenya and Tanzania, where the events surrounding "The Day We Saw the Elephant" occurred. Her poems have appeared most recently in *Barnabe Mountain Review, Beside the Sleeping Maiden, Americas Review,* and *The Birmingham Review.*

Douglas Lawder spent time in Cozumel in a middle–class Mexican neighborhood where he was able to live and write in modest circumstances. It was there that he met Lourdes, the Mayan woman who worked at the bank, helped him get checks cashed, and eventually became his student of English. His new book *Binoculars* was winner of the 1999 Stevens Award.

David Lloyd teaches at Le Moyne College, Syracuse, New York. His poems, stories, articles, and interviews have appeared in numerous publications, including *Denver Quarterly, Poetry Wales, Planet,* and *TriQuarterly.* His anthology, *The Urgency of Identity: Contemporary English–Language Poetry from Wales* (Northwestern University Press), appeared in 1994. The son of Welsh immigrants, he lived in Wales for two years and continues to be a frequent visitor.

Jeff Loo, a Philadelphia–born poet/writer, teaches creative writing at the Community College of Philadelphia. He has published in *Many Mountains Moving, Crab Orchard Review, Rampike, Southern Poetry Review, dlSorient,*

Green Mountain Review, and elsewhere.

Leza Lowitz is editor of award-winning anthologies of Japanese women's poetry, *A Long Rainy Season* and *Other Side River,* and author of *Old Ways to Fold New Paper.* Awarded a PEN Syndicated Fiction Award and the *1999 Japanophile* Fiction Prize, Ms. Lowitz has also received NEA, NEH, and California Arts Council grants. She lived in Tokyo from 1990 to 1994. Her new book is *Yoga Poems: Lines to Unfold By.*

Diane Sher Lutovich, a partner in a training and consulting business, is a former co-president of the Marin Poetry Center. She has been published in many journals, including *The Atlanta Review,* and *Mediphors.* Her trip to India turned her world upside down.

Tom McCarthy is a freelance writer. The former editor of *The Tenderloin Times* and contributor to the *Phnom Penh Cambodia Post,* he lives in San Francisco with his wife and daughter. His journalism, poetry, and essays have appeared in a wide variety of periodicals.

Marjorie Maddox received the Sage Graduate Fellowship from Cornell University and her MFA in 1989. She is now an associate professor of English at Lock Haven University in Pennsylvania. She has published one book, four chapbooks, and over 250 poems in literary journals. Andrew Hudgins said about her first book *Perpendicular As I* (winner of the 1994 Sandstone Poetry Book Award), "Maddox returns again and again to the ways body becomes landscape and landscape becomes body, internal and external repeatedly merging with one another."

Margaret Mantle is a British-born journalist, author, and poet who now lives in Evanston, Illinois. She was raised in Kent—the garden of England—and trained and worked as a reporter and feature writer on London's Fleet Street before embarking on some rather exotic, marriage-induced travels, which included time living in Russia and Argentina, before coming to the United States twenty years ago. Her latest poetry credits include *California Quarterly* and *Troubadour.* She has recently been nominated for a Pushcart Prize.

William Wei-Yi Marr has published twelve volumes of poetry, eleven of them in his native Chinese language, and several books of translations and anthologies. His poems have appeared in over eighty anthologies and are widely read in Taiwan, China, Hong Kong, Southeast Asia, as well as in the United States. Some of his poems have been translated into many European and Oriental languages. His book of poems in English, *Autumn Window,* was published in 1996 by Arbor Hill Press.

Hallie Moore, a poet and college English teacher, is currently enrolled in

Antioch University's MFA program in Los Angeles. She was living in Brazil and had traveled to Peru to visit the Incan ruins at Machu-Picchu near Cuzco when this poem occurred.

Carol Nolde teaches at Westfield Senior High School, Westfield, New Jersey, and is on the editorial board of *Merlyn's Pen*, a national magazine of student writing. Her poems have appeared in such publications as *Hellas, The MacGuffin, Adirondac, Ekphrasis, Blue Mountain, California State Poetry Quarterly*, and, most recently, *Whetstone*.

Sandra Olson has spent the last fourteen years travelling whenever possible, doing volunteer work and wandering through Europe, the Middle East, and Asia. She spent two summers in Russia and went to Nepal in 1998 to work with a group called Educate the Children. Her fiction and poetry have appeared in such magazines as *Visions International, ARK/angel Review, Kalliope, New South Review, Slipstream, Mediphors,* and *Parting Gifts*.

June Owens, a native of New York City, now lives and writes in central Florida. Her poetry, book reviews and nonfiction have most recently appeared in *Atlanta Review, Buckle &, The Caribbean Writer, Manoa, Rhino, Snowy Egret, Tirra Lirra*, and in many anthologies. Her book *Tree Line* and a chapbook *The Mask of Agamemnon* were released in 1999.

Joseph Powell teaches in the English Department at Central Washington University. In 1996, and again in 1999, he and his family spent three months teaching and traveling in Greece. His most recent book of poems, *Getting Here*, was published in 1997 by the Quarterly Review of Literature.

Maria Quinn has spent her life traveling and translating a rambler's experience into poetry and short stories. The landscape, the people and the rich cultural history of the Andes Mountains have made a lasting impression on her.

David Radavich's latest collection, *By the Way: Poems over the Years* (Buttonwood Press, 1998), includes a series of Egyptian poems based on his 1996 trip to the ancient, enchanting city of Alexandria. He has also had plays performed widely from New York to Los Angeles and has published articles on poetry, drama, and the contemporary writing scene.

John Calvin Rezmerski, writer-in-residence at Gustavus College in St. Peter, Minnesota, has received a National Endowment for the Arts fellowship, among other awards. Since writing "A Gift of Two Stones," he has seen Tiananmen and the Great Wall. His latest book *What Do I Know? New and Selected Poems* is being released by Holy Cow!

Elisavietta Ritchie's latest book *In Haste I Write You This Note: Stories* *and Half–Stories* won the Washington Writers' Publishing House's premiere fiction prize. *Flying Time: Stories & Half–Stories* contains four PEN Syndicated Fiction winners. Her poetry collections include: *The Arc of the Storm, Elegy for the Other Woman, Wild Garlic, Raking The Snow,* and *Tightening the Circle Over Eel Country.* Ms Ritchie has edited *The Dolphin's Arc: Endangered Creatures of the Sea.* Her poems have been published in *Poetry, American Scholar,* and the *New York Times,* as well as numerous other publications in North America and abroad.

Elliot Richman has won NEA and New York Foundation for the Arts Fellowships in Poetry. He has published four collections, the latest, *FRANZ KAFKA'S DAUGHTER MEETS THE EVIL NAZI EMPIRE!!! The Heroism of Roaches: Holocaust-tainted Poems,* 1999, was published by Grey Boyd's Asylum Arts Press.

Tom Roby and his wife Mary have traveled the globe searching out curricular materials for their Humanities and Religious Studies courses. But they have gone for their own joy of discovering other persons and places, and of finding, in unexpected ways, themselves. Tom wrote the two poems in this volume on a 1987 trip to Malta (megalithic temples), Venice (music), and Valcomonica (prehistoric rock art).

Paulette Roeske traveled for several weeks in Sicily in 1990 on an Illinois Arts Council Literature Fellowship, documenting her experiences through poems. Some of these appear in her second collection, *Divine Attention,* which won the 1996 Carl Sandburg Book Award for Poetry. Her latest collection of poems, *Anvil, Clock, and Last,* is forthcoming from Louisiana State University Press.

Bertha Rogers's poems have appeared in many journals, including *Many Mountains Moving, Connecticut Review, Nimrod,* and *Yankee.* She has received fellowships from Hawthornden Castle International Writers Retreat (Scotland) and the MacDowell Colony. Her poetry collections include *Sleeper, You Wake* and *For the Girl Buried in the Peat Bog.* Her translation of Beowulf is being published by Birch Brook Press.

Rose Rosberg was a high school librarian and practicing poet when she wrote the poems included here after visits made to Bali and Machu Picchu during school vacations. Her three volumes of poetry are *Trips—Without LSD; Breathe In, Breathe Out;* and *The Country of Connections.* Her work has been published in many literary journals.

Willa Schneberg worked, from 1992-93, for the United Nations Transitional Authority. She is a documentary photographer and clay sculptor, and has had two one-woman exhibitions in Portland, Oregon, relating to her time in Cambodia. Her volume of poetry entitled *Box Poems* was published by Alice James Books. Recently, she was awarded the Walt Morey Fellowship in Poetry from Oregon Literary Arts and a grant from the Money for Women/Barbara Deming Memorial Fund. She has two poems in the Jan/Feb 2000 issue of *American Poetry Review*. She is a Fellow in Poetry at the Tyrone Guthrie Center at Annaghmakerrig, Ireland.

Darrell g.h. Schramm lived in Cartagena, Colombia for two years and has traveled twice to Scotland, his favorite country. His poems, stories, and essays have appeared in over a hundred publications. He teaches at the University of San Francisco.

Don Schofield, who was born in Nevada and raised in California, has lived in Greece since 1980. He currently teaches literature and creative writing at the University of La Verne, Athens Campus. His poems and translations have appeared in various American and international journals.

Sharon Scholl, a Professor of Humanities at Jacksonville University, is devoted to primal cultures, primarily Indian, African and native Caribbean. Sharon is a performing musician, an avid traveler, and the author of two collections of poetry.

Dr. M. P. A. Sheaffer is a Professor at Millersville University of Pennsylvania. A member of the Poetry Society of America, she has edited four anthologies of poetry and has authored *Moonrocks and Metaphysical Turnips* and *Lacquer Birds and Leaves of Brass*. A third volume will be published in England in 2000. More than 400 of Dr. Sheaffer's poems have appeared in national and international literary journals. She has also won top prizes in both national and international poetry contests.

Enid Shomer's work appears in *The New Yorker, Atlantic Monthly, Paris Review, Poetry, New Criterion,* and many more. She is the author of three poetry books and of *Imaginary Men,* winner of the Iowa Prize and the LSU/Southern Review Prize, both awarded annually for the best first fiction collection by an American author.

Vivian Shipley is the Connecticut State University Distinguished Professor. The Editor of *Connecticut Review,* she teaches at Southern Connecticut State University. Raised in Kentucky, Ms. Shipley has traveled and published widely. She is the recipient of numerous poetry awards, including the 1997 Lucille Medwick Award from the Poetry Society of America.

Layle Silbert, a writer of short stories and poems as well as a photographer, often incorporates material from her travels into her writing. She was with her husband on their way back from a United Nations mission in Pakistan when their plane landed unexpectedly in Basra.

Floyd Skloot spent the summer of 1994 as a writer–in–residence at the Heinrich Boll Cottage on Ireland's Achill Island. His books of poetry include *Music Appreciation* and *The Evening Light*. His work has appeared in *Atlantic Monthly, Harper's, Poetry, Hudson Review,* and many other magazines in America and Europe. Mr. Skloot has also published three novels and a book of essays.

Laurence Snydal is a poet, musician, and professional cook. His poetry has appeared in such magazines as *Blue Unicorn, Caperock, Lyric,* and *Gulf Stream*. He has also published two non-fiction books, guides for new fathers. "Visiting the Dead" was the result of a European trip in 1993. When he returned with stories and photos, a friend remarked, "All you did was visit dead people." Somewhat apt.

Joseph A. Soldati of Portland, Oregon, is a retired English professor who has traveled a good portion of the globe, including Greece and Italy and the sites referred to in his poem. He is the author of two poetry books—*O Poetry! Oh Poesìa! Poems of Oregon and Peru* (1997) and *Making My Name* (1992).

Dale Sprowl lives in Newport Beach, California with her husband and three children. As a teacher/consultant for the UCI Writing Project, she teaches and contributes to their academic books. Her poems have appeared in *Pearl, A New Song,* and *Ancient Paths*. She has traveled to Israel, Tahiti, and to the Ukraine on a mission trip visiting hospitals and orphanages.

B. A. St. Andrews teaches creative writing and various traditional and medical humanities courses at SUNY/Health Science Center in Syracuse, New York. She is published in *The Paris Review, Carolina Quarterly, Journal of the American Medical Association* and *The New Yorker.*

Cassie Premo Steele is an award winning and internationally published poet as well as an adjunct professor of comparative literature at the University of South Carolina. Her scholarly interests in Latina/o literature led her to Ecuador and Mexico, where "Dos Marias" and "Red is the Color of the Year" were written. She is also the editor of *Moon Days: Creative Writings about Menstruation* and the author of *We Heal From Memory: Sexton, Lorde, Anzaldúa and the Poetry of Witness,* forthcoming from St. Martin's Press.

Amy Stewart is a poet and writer living in Santa Cruz, California. Her poetry has appeared in a variety of literary journals, including *Puerto del Sol, Evansville Review,* and *Brooklyn Review*. Her first book *From the Ground Up: The Making of a Garden* is being released by Algonquin Books.

Joy E. Stocke is co-founder of the Meridian Writers Collective. She travels frequently to Greece and Turkey and is working on a series of essays based on her travels. Her book of poems, *The Cave of the Bear*, set on the island of Crete, was recently published by Pella Press.

Ann Struthers lived in Syria for two years, teaching at the University of Aleppo on a Fulbright Fellowship. Enriched with all the historical sites, she has written a number of poems about them. Syria has fantastic ruins, including the *tell* (hill) of Ain Dara where the Japanese are excavating the temple of Ishtar.

Thea Sullivan is a San Francisco poet and teacher of writing whose work has appeared in numerous journals, including *Calyx, 13th Moon, Rain City Review,* and *Switched-on Gutenberg*. She and her husband honeymooned in Thailand, a trip which gave rise to the poem, "On the Chao Phraya, Bangkok."

Gladys Swan's recent travels have taken her to Maya ruins in Mexico and Guatemala, where she teaches a fiction workshop in Antiqua. She has published two novels and four collections of short stories, the latest being, *A Visit to Strangers*. Her poetry has appeared in many journals, including *The Sewanee Review*.

Christine Swanberg is a writing teacher whose summers often give her time to explore exotic places. She spent an entire summer in Central America. Christine has published over 200 poems and five collections of poetry. The joys, trials, triumphs, and epiphanies of travel have informed many of her poems. Her husband of 27 years is also a teacher and travel photographer.

Ann Sylvester received her MFA from the University of Arizona in 1997. Her poems have appeared in *Blue Violin, Earth's Daughters, Quantum Tao,* and *Ruah*. She is a grand prize winner for the poem, "The River," which was choreographed for the 1999 Dancing Poetry Festival in San Francisco. She has lived in Jerusalem, Tucson, and Northern California. She teaches creative writing in Berkeley and Walnut Creek, California.

Kathy Kennedy Tapp's poems have appeared in many literary journals, including *Wisconsin Academy Review, Fox Cry Review,* and *Skylark*. She is also the author of several young adult novels. While attending a conference on myth at Trinity College in Dublin, she visited Newgrange and felt the power, the enigma, the age, and the silence of the ancient chamber.

Susan Terris' book *Curved Space* was published in 1998. In 1999 she had two poetry books released: *Eye of the Holocaust* and *Angels of Bataan*. Other recent books are *Killing into the Comfort Zone* and *Nell's Quilt*. Her many journal publications include *The Antioch Review, The Midwest Quar-*

terly, Painted Bride Quarterly, Missouri Review, Nimrod, Southern California Anthology, and *The Southern Poetry Review.* In 1998 Ms. Terris was nominated for a Pushcart Pize, won first place in four poetry competitions, and was a second place winner or finalist in ten other national competitions.

Lorraine Tolliver is a professor in Compton, California. Her short stories and poems have appeared in *American Poets and Poetry, Poetry/LA, Los, New Mirage, Grain, Aurorean, Aim, Contemporary Books, Papier-Maché, Forum,* and others.

Michael Waters is Professor of English at Salisbury State University on the Eastern Shore of Maryland. His six books of poetry include *Green Ash, Red Maple, Black Gum; Bountiful; The Burden Lifters;* and *Anniversary of the Air.* BOA will release his *New and Selected Poems* this year. He has been the recipient of a Fellowship in Creative Writing from the National Endowment for the Arts, three Individual Artist Awards from the Maryland State Arts Council, and two Pushcart Prizes. He has traveled widely, spending time in Greece, Thailand, Costa Rica, Romania, Belize, Iraq and other countries.

Anthony Russell White is a pilgrim, poet, genealogist, and healer. He has been writing poetry (again) since 1992. A poetic high point was a visit to the tomb of Jeladuddin Rumi at Konya, Turkey. He continues to be awed by Rumi's poetry.

David Whyte grew up among the hills and valleys of Yorkshire, England. He holds a degree in Marine Zoology, and has worked as a Naturalist guide in the Galapagos Islands, led anthropological and natural history expeditions in Peru, Bolivia, and Chile, and subsequently traveled India and the hinterlands of Nepal. He now lives at sea level on Whidbey Island, Washington, reading and lecturing throughout the United States, Canada and Europe.

Carolyne Wright was in Calcutta from 1986–88 on an Indo–U.S. Subcommission Fellowship; and from 1989–91 in Dhaka, Bangladesh, on a Fulbright Senior Research Fellowship, to collect and translate the work of 20th–century Bengali women poets and writers for two anthologies in process: *A Bouquet of Roses on the Burning Ground: Poetry by Bengali Women,* and *Crossing the Seasonal River: Stories of Bengal by Women.* She is also working on an investigative memoir of her experiences in Chile during the ill-fated presidency of Salvador Allende, *The Road to Isla Negra,* which has already received the PEN/Jerard Fund Award and the Crossing Boundaries Award from *International Quarterly.* During the year in Chile, she also travelled in Brazil and the Andean countries of Bolivia and Peru. Her publications include six books of poetry, a volume of essays, and three collections of poetry translated from

Spanish and Bengali.

Bill Yake spends daytime hours studying streams and estuaries for the state of Washington—practicing being fully native in his homeland. Over the past three years his experiences of exotic lands have stretched from previous explorations of Italy, Vienna, and Tunisia, south and west to China, Japan, Papua New Guinea and northern Australia. He has published poems in thirteen states, one province, and the District of Columbia.

Marilyn Zuckerman has published three books of poetry, *Personal Effects*, (along with the work of two other poets), *Monday Morning Movie*, and *Poems of the Sixth Decade*. Her poems appear in such literary journals as *New York Quarterly, The Little Magazine, Nimrod, Pig Iron,* and *Ourselves Growing Older,* as well as the anthology *Claiming the Spirit Within.* Ms. Zuckerman has received a PEN Syndicated Fiction Award and has placed short stories in several anthologies.

Acknowledgements

Grateful acknowledgement is made to the following publications where some of the poems in this volume first appeared or have been published.

Barfield, Steven: "An Egyptian Evening," *Black Moon,* Issue 2, 1997.
Barfield, Steven: "Lorca at the Wall," *Black Moon,* Issue 3, 1998.
Bargen, Walter: "The Civilized Sacrifice," *Pleiades,* Volume 18, Number 2, 1998.
Bargen, Walter: "Russian Parliament 8/20/91," *The Cape Rock,* Volume 30, Number 1, Spring 1995.
Bayer, Deanne: "Megaliths," first appeared as "Stonehenge," in *The Sulphur River Literary Review,* Volume XII, Number 2, Autumnal Equinox, 1996.
Beban, Richard: "First Anniversary Pantoum," *I Burn For You,* The Inevitable Press, 1999. Reprinted by permission of the author.
Beban, Richard: "For My Best Friend, Who Has Seen Miracles," *Fried Eggs With Lace: A Family Poem,* Canned Spaghetti Press, 1996. Reprinted by permission of the author.
Beban, Richard: "Our Lady of the Pigeons," *SOLO Magazine,* Issue 3, May 1999.
Beban, Richard: "What the Heart Weighs (In the Catacombs, Paris 1997)," *I Burn For You,* The Inevitable Press, 1999. Reprinted by permission of the author.
Berger, Bruce: "Recalling San Ignacio," *Aspen Leaves,* Volume 2, Number 2, 1974.
Blaker, Margaret: "Pacal's Tomb," *Archaeology,* Volume 51, Number 1, January 1988.
Blaker, Margaret: "Underworld Palace Scene with Beheading," *Archaeology,* Volume 51, Number 1, January 1988.
Bolz, Jody: "Wayang," *The Women's Review of Books,* Spring 2000.
Buckley, W. K.: "Stone Lemons," *81 Mygrations,* Fithian Press, 1998. Reprinted by permission of the author.
Byrne, Deborah: "Shadow Poem," *Dream International Quarterly,* Issue 28, Fall 1999.
Byrne, Deborah: "The Spanish Boys at The Hotel Manx," first appeared in *The Crab Creek Review,* Summer/Autumn 1998; reprinted in *Ibbetson St.* Volume 1, Issue 1 May 1999; reprinted in *Rockhurst Review: A Journal of Fine Arts,* Volume 12, Summer 1999; reprinted in *Cold Drill,* 1999; reprinted in *Acid Angel,* Issue 4, 2000, Glasgow, Scotland; reprinted in *Mandrake Poetry Review,* Summer 2000, Gliwice, Poland.
Casebeer, Linda: "Through Breezes of Chanta Palms," first appeared as "River" in *Hawaii Pacific Review,* Volume 12, 1998.
Cherry, Kelly: "At Night Your Mouth," *Natural Theology,* Louisiana State University Press, 1983. Reprinted by permission of Louisiana State University Press.
Cherry, Kelly: "Livadiya Palace: Site of the Yalta Conference," *Death and Transfiguration,* Louisiana State University Press, 1997. Reprinted by permission of Louisiana State University Press.
Cherry, Kelly: "Plans for a House in Latvia," *Natural Theology,* Louisiana State University Press 1983. Reprinted by permission of Louisiana State University Press.
Cherry, Kelly: "Report from an Unnamed City," *God's Loud Hand,* Louisiana State University Press 1993. Reprinted by permission of Louisiana State University Press.
Conlon, Christopher: "At the Great Zimbabwe Ruins," *Santa Barbara Review,* Summer 1996.
Conlon, Christopher: "The Ballroom," *Peace Corps Writers and Readers,* July 1995.
Conlon, Christopher: "Soweto," *Wind,* Fall 1994.
Crisick, Maureen Micus: "La Paz," *Iowa Woman,* Volume 12, Number 3, Autumn 1992.

Crisick, Maureen Micus: "Road to Santipur" Reprinted from *THE AMERICAN SCHOLAR*, Volume 67, Number 1, Winter 1998. Copyright 1998 Maureen Micus Crisick. Reprinted by permission of the publishers.

Crisick, Maureen Micus: "Without Sun, Without Language," *San Francisco State University Review*, Spring 1995.

Dickson, John: "Echoes of a Native Land," *Poetry*, Volume CLXIV, Number 3, June 1994.

Doyle, James: "The Well of Sacrifice," *Sandscripts*, Issue 14, 1988.

Elyshevitz, Alan: "Poland, 1990," *Poems and Plays*, Number 3, Spring/Summer 1996.

Engle, Diane: "Creation at Stonehenge," first appeared as "Stonehenge," in *ELF (Eclectic Literary Forum)*, Volume 8, Number 3/4, 1998.

Fammerée, Richard: "Asleep in Ireland," *Lessons of Water and Thirst*, Collage Press, 2000. Reprinted by permission of the author.

Fammerée, Richard: "Eulogia," *Lessons of Water and Thirst*, Collage Press, 2000. Reprinted by permission of the author.

Fammerée, Richard: "Evora (a song)," *Lessons of Water and Thirst*, Collage Press, 2000. Reprinted by permission of the author.

Gibson, Stephen: "The Coming of Agriculture," *Ohio Journal*, Volume 9, Number 1, Spring/Summer 1985.

Gilgun, John: "Mayan Pyramid, Yucatan Peninsula," first appeared as "Shaman Song From a Mayan Peninsula" in *Shaman's Drum: a Journal of Experiential Shamanism*, Number 41, Spring 1996.

Gill, Michael: "Laguna Los Tres Cruces," *Pemmican*, Number 6, 1997.

Gillespie, Netta: "Monument: Avebury Stone Circle," *Matrix VI*, Red Herring Press, 1982. Reprinted by permission of the author.

Green, Daniel: "Night Vision," first appeared in *Sensation*, January 1993; reprinted in *Poetic Eloquence*, January 1994; reprinted in *Simply Words*, November 1995; reprinted in *Fauquier*, June 1998.

Greenway, William: "At Arthur's Stone," *Simmer Dim*, by William Greenway, The University of Akron Press, 1999. Reprinted by permission of The University of Akron Press.

Greenway, William: "Self–Burial," *Simmer Dim*, by William Greenway, The University of Akron Press, 1999. Reprinted by permission of The University of Akron Press.

Harrington, Jonathan: "Rainy Season," *Slant*, Summer 1988.

Harrington, Jonathan: "Ruins," *South Florida Poetry Review*, Winter, 1988.

Harrington, Jonathan: "Smile," *Without Halos*, Volume 9, Fall 1991.

Holloway, Glenna: "The Enlightened One," *Poet*, Volume 5, Number 1, 1993; reprinted in *Japanophile*, Volume 18, Number 1, Winter 1994.

Iddings, Kathleen: "Taormina, Sicily," *Selected and New Poems, 1980–1990*, West Anglia Publications, 1990. Reprinted by permission of the author.

Kanter, Carol: "Scapegoats," *2000: Here's to Humanity*, People's Press, 2000.

Karrer, Pearl: "Printmaking: Wiping an Inked Plate," *National Poetry Competition Winners, 1989*, Chester H Jones Foundation, 1989.

Keyes, Claire: "Dolemen on the Kilkenny Road," *Talking River Review*, Winter 1999.

Kingston, Katie: "A Short Way," *They recommend this place*, editor Gretchin Lair, by Women's Studies Program, University of Southern Colorado, 1999. Reprinted by permission of the publisher and author.

Knoepfle, John: "dysert o–dea," *New Letters*, Volumer 65, Number 3, 1999.

Knoepfle, John: "notes from a journey," *Argestes*, 2000.

Lawder, Douglas W.: "Translating Lourdes," *Way Station,* Number 4.

Lloyd, David: "Transformations of Stone," *The Anglo–Welsh Review,* Number 84, 1986.

Loo, Jeffrey: "In Kamakura (Japan)," first appeared in another form in *Raven Chronicles,* Volume 4, Number 2, Spring 1995.

Lowitz, Leza: "At the Senbitsuka," first appeared in *Japan Environment Monitor,* Volume 5, Number 2, 1992; reprinted in *Katanogahura,* Number 45, 1998; reprinted in *Old Ways to Fold New Paper,* 1996. Reprinted by permission of Wandering Mind Books.

Lowitz, Leza: "Berlin Wall," *Poetry Flash,* November 1989; reprinted in *Old Ways to Fold New Paper,* 1996. Reprinted by permission of Wandering Mind Books.

Lowitz, Leza: "Rising and Falling," *Old Ways to Fold New Paper,* Wandering Mind Books, 1996. Reprinted by permission of Wandering Mind Books.

Lowitz, Leza: "The Seamstress," first appeared in *Poetry Kanto,* Number 11, Summer 1995; reprinted in *Old Ways to Fold New Paper,* 1996. Reprinted by permission of Wandering Mind Books.

McCarthy, Tom: "Phnom Penh Street," *2000: Here's to Humanity,* People's Press, 2000.

McCarthy, Tom: "Prosthesis Factory in Phnom Penh," *Green Fuse,* Spring 1995.

Marr, William Wei-Yi: "The Great Wall," *Autumn Window,* Arbor Hill Press, 1991. Reprinted by permission of the author.

Moore, Hallie: "Andean Snapshot," *Borderlands: Texas Poetry Review,* Number 8, Spring/Summer 1996.

Olson, Sandra: "Of Barracks and Bee Stings," *Sheila Na Gig,* Number 11.

Owens, June: "The Boy Who Dreamed of Building Pompeii," *Prize Poems of the National Federation of State Poetry Societies, 1992,* edited by Russell Ferrall, 1993 by National State Poetry Societies, Inc. Reprinted by permission of the author.

Powell, Joseph: "Easter in Aegina," *Aegean Dialogues,* March Street Press. Reprinted by permission of the author.

Powell, Joseph: "The Theatre at Epidaurus," *Aegean Dialogues,* March Street Press. Reprinted by permission of the author.

Quinn, Maria: "On a Plane from Cuzco," *Chachalaca,* Spring 2000.

Rezmerski, John Calvin: "A Gift of Two Stones, for Mr. Liang," *What Do I Know?* Holy Cow! Press, 2000. Reprinted by permission of the author.

Richman, Elliot: "The Kiss," *Asylum Annual, 1995,* ed. Greg Boyd, Asylum Arts, 1995. Reprinted by permission of the author.

Ritchie, Elisavietta: "In Kraljevo," *Raking The Snow,* Washington Writers Publishing House, 1982. Reprinted by permission of the author.

Ritchie, Elisavietta: "In Transit" first appeared in *Island,* 1997; reprinted in *The Ledge,* 1998; reprinted in *Canadian Women's Studies,* 1998; reprinted in *Soundings,* 1998.

Ritchie, Elisavietta: "Reading the Stones," first appeared in *Quantum Tao,* Volume 1, Number 1; reprinted in *The Arc of the Storm,* Signal Books, 1998. Reprinted by permission of the author.

Ritchie, Elisavietta: "Sarajevo," an earlier version of part one first appeared in *Christian Science Monitor,* 1990; part two first appeared in *Home Planet News,* 1990; reprinted in *Raking The Snow,* Washington Writers' Publishing House, 1982; current version reprinted in *The Arc of the Storm,* Signal Books, 1998. Reprinted by permission of the author.

Ritchie, Elisavietta: "Them," first appeared in *Outsiders/ Sunk Island Review,* Issue 9, 1994; reprinted in *Amelia,* 1994; reprinted in *The Arc of the Storm,* Signal Books, 1998. Reprinted by permission of the author.

Ritchie, Elisavietta: "To Ride the White Camel," first appeared in *Poet Lore,* 1985; reprinted in *The Arc of the Storm,* Signal Books, 1998. Reprinted by permission of the author.

Roeske, Paulette: "The Body Can Ascend No Higher," first appeared in *Chester H. Jones Foundation National Poetry Competition Winners, 1990,* Chester H Jones Foundation, 1990; reprinted in *The Body Can Ascend No Higher,* Illinois Writers, Inc., 1992; reprinted in *Divine Attention,* Louisiana State University Press, 1995. Reprinted by permission of the author.

Rogers, Bertha: "The Barber Surgeon's Death," *Sleeper, You Wake,* Edwin Mellen Press, 1991. Reprinted by permission of the author.

Rosberg, Rose: "Ingenue in Bali," first appeared in *Manhattan Poetry Review,* Number 5, Summer/Fall 1985; reprinted in *The Country of Connections,* University Editions, 1993. Reprinted by permission of the author.

Rosberg, Rose: "Pressage at Machu Picchu," *Voices International,* Volume 12, Spring 1997.

Schofield, Donald: "I Don't Know the Local," *Southern Poetry Review.*

Schramm, Darrell g.h.: "Eileen Munda," *Albatross,* Number 8, 1992.

Shipley, Vivian: "A Woman Can Live by Bread Alone, *Nightsun,* Issue 17, Fall 1997.

Shomer, Enid: "From the Wailing Wall," first appeared in *Kalliope;* reprinted in *This Close to Earth,* University of Arkansas Press, 1992. Reprinted by permission of University of Arkansas Press.

Shomer, Enid: "In the Viennese Style," first appeared in *Poetry;* reprinted in *Black Drum,* University of Arkansas Press, 1997. Reprinted by permission of University of Arkansas Press.

Shomer, Enid: "On Jekyll Island," *The New Criterion;* reprinted in *This Close to the Earth,* University of Arkansas Press, 1992. Reprinted by permission of University of Arkansas Press.

Shomer, Enid: "To the Field of Reeds," *This Close to the Earth,* University of Arkansas Press, 1992. Reprinted by permission of University of Arkansas Press.

Silbert, Layle: "Not To Be in Basra," *U.S.1 Worksheets,* Number 36–37, 1997.

Skloot, Floyd: "Dawn at Sligo Bay," *Blue Mesa Review,* Number 9, 1997.

Sprowl, Dale: "The Western Wall," *A New Song,* Volume 4, Number 2, Summer 1999.

St. Andrews, B. A.: "Aztecs," *Chaminade Literary Review,* Volume 14 & 15, Srping/Fall 1994.

Stocke, Joy: "The Rug Dealer," first appeared as "Red" in *Patterson Literary Review,* Number 28, Fall 1999; reprinted in *The Cave of the Bear,* Pella Press, 1999. Reprinted by permission of the author.

Swanberg, Christine: "Stone with Hole," *RHINO,* Volume 4, Number 2, 1985.

Sylvester, Ann: "The River," *Ruah,* Volume VIII, 1998. Grand Prize for the Dancing Poetry Festival Contest, San Francisco, 1999.

Terris, Susan: "On Seeing the Dead Walk," *Sow's Ear Poetry Review,* Volume X, Number 2, July 1999.

Terris, Susan: "Shadows of Moremi," *The Midwest Quarterly,* Volume XXXIX, Number 2, Winter 1998.

Waters, Michael: "The Lost Civilization," first appeared in *Carolina Quarterly,* Volume 41, Number 1, Fall 1990; reprinted in *Bountiful,* Carnegie Mellon, 1992. Reprinted by permission of the aurthor.

Waters, Michael: "Night in the Tropics 1858–59?," *Poetry,* Volume CLVI, Number 5, August 1990; reprinted in *Bountiful,* Carnegie Mellon, 1992. Reprinted by permission of the author.

Waters, Michael: "Passion Conch," *The Burden Lifters,* Carnegie Mellon University, 1989. Reprinted by permission of the author.

Whyte, David: "The Faces at Braga," *Where Many Rivers Meet,* Many Rivers Press, 1990. Reprinted by permission of the author.

Wright, Carolyne: "The Conjure Woman," *Kayak,* 1983.

Wright, Carolyne: "Eulene Between Acts," first appeared as "Intraludus Euleneiae" in *International Quarterly,* Volume 2, Number 3, 1995.
Wright, Carolyne: "The Miracle Room," *Open Places,* Number 35, Spring/Summer 1983.
Wright, Carolyne: "The Room," *The Iowa Review,* Volume 28, Number 2, 1998.
Yake, Bill: "Michaelskirche, Vienna," *Seattle Review,* Volume VI, Number 1, 1993.

Index

Aachen, Germany, 243
Achill Island, Ireland, 38
Aegina, Greece, 280–81
Africa, 76–77 110, 111, 163–64, 181, 194–95, 266
Afrin, Syria, 70,
Aghia Marina, Aegina, Greece, 281
Aguas Calientes, Peru, 121
Ain Dara, Syria, 70, 71
Alaska, 227–28
Alausi, Ecuador, 57–58
Aleppo, Syria, 71
Alexandria, Egypt, 22, 182
Alfacar, Spain, 153
Alhambra, Granada, Spain, 153, 276
Amazon River, 218, 219, 220
Andalusia, Spain, 153
Andes Mountains, 57–58, 59–60, 61–62, 175, 176–77, 178, 250, 251–52
Annapurna, Himalayas of Nepal, 93, 258, 260
Arabia, 73
Aran Islands, Ireland, 196–97
Arctic Regions, 85–86, 221–22, 267
Argentina, 252
Arno River, Italy, 170
Arthur's Stone, Wales, 112–13
Aswan Dam, Egypt, 264–65
Athens, Greece, 98–99
Atlantis, 100
Auschwitz, Poland 154
Australia, 14, 144–45

Austria, 240, 243
Avebury Stone Circle, Wiltshire, England, 44, 244
Avranches, France, 211
Bahia, Brazil, 117–18, 179–80
Baja California Sur, 20–21, 215
Bali, Indonesia, 128, 268
Bandung, Indonesia, 128
Bangkok, Thailand, 167
Bangladesh, 131
Baranquilla, Colombia, 158
Basra, Iraq, 29
Les Baux, France 210
Bayon Temple, Anghor Thom, Cambodia, 135
Belgrade, Serbia, 125
Belize, 22, 285
Berkeley, California, 73
Berlin Wall, 81, 155, 241
Bermuda Triangle, 203
Birkenau, Poland 154
Bizen, Okayama, Japan, 138
Black Sea, 148
Blue Mosque, Istanbul, Turkey, 286
Bombay, India, 23
Bosnia, 134, 151–52
Bosra, Syria, 71
Botswana, Africa, 110, 181, 194
Braga Monastery, Nepal 259–60
Brazil, 117–18, 163–64, 179-80
British Museum, London, 234
Brujenkhola, Nepal, 91
Budapest, Hungary, 241

INDEX

Bülbül Mountain, Turkey, 68
Bulgaria, 183
Burren, County Clare, Ireland 273–74
Burry, Wales, 112
Bytom, Poland, 154
Cabo San Lucas, Mexico, 214–15
Cairo, 29, 72, 264–65
Calanais Standing Stones, Lewis Island, Scotland, 39
California, 189, 190–91, 237
Cambodia, 133–34, 135, 173–74
Cambodiana Hotel, Phnom Penh, Cambodia, 135
Canada, 200
Canyon de Muerte, Arizona, 51
Capo di Ponte, Italy, 236
Caribbean Region, 105, 141–42, 164, 203–04, 206, 207, 208
Cartagena, Colombia, 158
Castellammare del Golfo, Italy, 115
Catacombs, Paris, 238–39
Cecil Hotel, Alexandria, Egypt, 182
Cefn Bryn, Wales, 112
Chao Phraya River, Thailand, 167
Charles Bridge, Prague, 192
Chartres Cathedral, France, 286
Chicago, 171–72
Chichén Itzá, Yucatan, 22, 52, 248–49
Chile, 160–62
China, 78–79, 80, 81
Cholla Province, South Korea, 138
Church of San Zeno, Verona, Italy, 65
Coba, Quintana Roo, Mexico, 56
Colombia, 158
Connaught (Connacht), Ireland, 270
Convento dei Cappuccini, Palermo, Italy, 242
County Clare, Ireland, 274
Cozumel, Yucatan, 119
Crete, Greece, 98–99, 185–86, 187–88
Crotone, Italy, 66

Cuzco, Peru, 59–60, 120, 121, 175, 176, 250
Cyprus, 28
Danube River, 241
Delhi, India, 102
Delphi, Greece, 64, 67, 98–99, 230–31
Dublin, Ireland, 271, 286
Dysert O'Dea, Ireland, 46
Dzibilchaltun, Yucatan, 53
Easter Island, 22
Ecuador, 57–58, 156, 178
Egypt, 72, 73, 74–75, 182, 234–35, 238, 264–65
Eileen Munda, Scotland, 94
Ellis Island, New York, 171, 226
England, 23, 41–42, 43, 44, 234–35, 244, 275
English Channel, 212
Ephesus, Turkey, 68
Epidaurus, Greece, 63
Evora, Portugal, 232–33
Fiesole, Italy, 65
Firenza, Italy, 170
Flanders Field, France, 160
Florence, Italy, 170
Florida, 122
Fortress Bellevedere, Florence, 170
France, 210, 211, 238–39, 243, 286
French Polynesia, 205
Fujiyama Mountain, Japan, 262
Ganges River, India, 131, 255–56
Georgia, 48
Giverney, France, 286
Glacier Bay, Alaska, 227–28
Glencoe, Scotland, 94
Granada, Spain, 153, 276
Great Rift Valley, Africa, 266
Great Wall, China, 78–79, 80, 81
Great Zimbabwe, Africa, 76–77
Greece, 30–31, 63, 64–65, 98–99, 184, 185–86, 187–88, 189, 280–81

Greenland, 267
Grenada, 105, 141–42
Guadeloupe Volcano, 168
Guatemala, 22
Hagar Qim, Malta, 278–79
Hakone Hills, Japan, 262
Halep (Aleppo), Syria, 71
Hanalei Valley Overlook, Princeville, Kauai, 140
Hanging Gardens of Babylon, 29
Hanoi, Vietnam, 109
Hawaii, 140, 209
Himalayas, 91–93, 257–58, 259–60
Hiroshima, Japan, 139
Horton–Dubingnon Plantation, Jekyll Island, Georgia, 48–49
Hotel Manx, San Francisco, 190–91
Hua Hin, Thailand, 103–04
Huayna Picchu Mountain, Peru, 121
Hungary, 32
India, 23, 101, 102, 255–56
Indonesia, 126–28, 247, 261, 268, 286
Inishgalloon, Ireland, 38
Ireland, 38, 45, 46, 196–97, 198–99, 213, 269, 270, 271–72, 273–74
Italy, 65, 115, 169, 170, 236, 242
Japan, 226, 229, 262, 263
Jekyll Island, Georgia, 48–49
Jerusalem, Israel, 82–83, 84, 217
Jiwali Mayi Mandir Temple, Muktinath, Nepal, 258
Jogjakarta, Indonesia, 261
Johannesburg, South Africa, 136
Jomosom, Nepal, 93, 258
Jordan, 28
Kalahari Desert, Africa, 181
Kamakura, Honshu, Japan, 262, 263
Kampa Island, Prague, 192
Karachi, Pakistan, 23
Kárpathos Island, Greece, 184

Kawaihae Coast, Hawaii, 209
Khajuraho, India, 101, 102
Kiev, Ukraine, 116
Mount Kilimanjaro, Tanzania, 217
Kilkenny, Ireland, 45
Knock na Rea, Sligo, Ireland, 270
Knossos, Crete, 186
Kohala Mountains, Hawaii, 209
Koricancha, Cuzco, Peru, 59–60
Kraków, Poland, 154
Kraljevo, Serbia, 125
Kuwait, 131–32
La Paz, Mexico, 216
Laguna Los Tres Cruces, Ecuador, 58
Lake Manyara Reserve, Tanzania, 111
Lake Superior, 81
Lappa, Crete, 185
Latvia, 106–107, 124
Lesbos, Greece, 30–31
Lewis, Outer Hebrides, Scotland, 39
Libyan Desert, 73
Liepaja, Latvia, 106
Lima, Peru, 176
Lisbon, 196
Livadiya Palace, Yalta, 148
Liverpool, England, 196
Lock Leven, Scotland, 94
London, England, 42, 234–35
Lookout Mountain, Tennessee, 220
Lough Keel, Ireland, 38
Ludsk, 226
Macedonia, 71
Machu Picchu, 60, 61, 120, 121, 175, 177
Malta, 278–79
Ma'lula, Syria, 71
Marseilles, France, 286
Masi Moto, Africa, 111
Maxwell Street, Chicago, Illinois, 171–72
Mendoza, Argentina, 252

Mendocino, California, 237
Mérida, Yucatan, Mexico, 34
Mexico City, 282–83
Mexico, 15, 22, 33–34, 53–54, 55, 56, 89–90, 119, 214–15, 216, 248–49, 282–83, 284, 285
Middle Passage, 163–64
Minnesota, 81
Mississippi Delta, 140
Mississippi, 50,
Monastery of the Angels, Karachi, Pakistan, 23
Moneda, Santiago, Chile, 160–62
Mont–Saint–Michel, France, 211–12
Monte Albán, Oaxaca, Mexico, 89–90
Moorèa, Tahiti, 205
Moremi, Africa, 110
Moscow, 116, 146, 149, 243
Mount Etna, Italy, 115
Mount Machha Puchhare, Nepal, 91
Mount Vesuvius, 25, 27
Muktinath, Nepal, 257–58
Muséo Nacional, Quito, Ecuador, 156
Mycenae, Greece, 64
Mytilene, Greece, 31
Nagasaki, Japan, 139
Nairobi, Kenya, 111
Nauplion, Greece, 63
Nepal, 91–93, 257–58, 259–60
Nevado Ampato Peak, Andes, 250
New Zealand, 143
Newfoundland, 200
Newgrange, Ireland, 269
New York City, Lower East Side, 226
Nile River, Egypt, 264–65
Normandy, France, 211–12
Nosso Senhor de Bomfim, Sao Salvador de Bahia, Brazil, 179-80
Nottingham, England, 275
Nove Mesto, Prague, Czech Republic, 150

Oaxaca, Mexico, 89-90,
Okavango River, Africa, 110
Olduvai Gorge, Africa, 266
Olymbos, Karpathos, Greece, 184
Olympia, Greece 65
Outer Hebrides, Scotland, 39
Paestum, Italy, 65
Pakistan, 23
Palenque, Chiapas, Mexico, 54, 55
Palermo, Italy, 242
Parguera, Puerto Rico, 206
Paris, 95–97, 238–39, 243
Peloponnese, Greece, 63
Penmaenmawr, Wales, 37
Pere Lachaise Cemetery, Paris, 95–97
Perm Region, Siberia, 146
Peru, 59–60, 61–62, 120, 175, 176, 218, 219, 220
Petrin Hill, Prague, 192
Phnom Penh, Cambodia, 133–34, 135, 173–74
Phosphorescent Bay, Puerto Rico, 206, 207, 208
Piazza San Marco, Venice, 169
Princeton Art Museum, 157
Pireaus, Greece, 281
Plaka, Athens, Greece, 98, 99
Pokhara, Nepal, 93
Pompeii, 25, 26
Port Arthur, Tasmania, 144–45
Portugal, 123, 232–33,
Potosí, Bolivia, 225
Poul na Brone Dolmen, County Clare, Ireland, 273–74
Prado Museum, Madrid, Spain, 122
Prague, 150, 192–93
Prambanan, Java, Indonesia, 261, 286
Puerto Rico, 206, 207, 208
Putacusi Mountain, Peru, 121
Pythagoras Academy, 66
Quillaloma, Ecuador, 57–58

Quintana Roo, Mexico, 285
Quito, Ecuador, 156
Red Sea, 266
Rethymnon, Crete, 186
Rhône River, France, 210
Ringstrasse, Vienna, Austria, 114
Roman Forum, 18
Rome, Italy, 18, 115
Russia, 116, 146, 149, 243
Sacred Valley of the Incas, Peru, 59–60
Sacsahuaman Fortress, Cuzco, Peru, 175
Sagres, Portugal, 122–23
Sahara Desert, Africa, 28
Salcantay Mountain, Peru, 121, 177
Salisbury Plain, England, 40, 41–42, 43
Salvador, Bahia, Brazil, 117–18
Samos, Greece, 65
San Francisco, 155, 190–91
San Ignacio, Mexico, 20
San Simeon, Syria, 69
Santiago, Chile, 160–62
Santorini, Greece, 100
Sao Salvador de Bahia, Brazil, 179–80
Sarajevo, Bosnia, 151–52
Scotland, 39, 94
Sea of Cortez, 215
Second Temple, Jerusalem, 83
Senbitsuka, Okayama, Japan, 138
Senso–ji Temple Asakusa, Tokyo, 226
Seti Khola, Nepal, 91
Sharm El Sheikh, 217
Sicily, Italy, 115, 242
Siena, Italy, 251
Siofok, Hungary, 32
Slievemore, Ireland, 38
Sligo Bay, Ireland, 213
Sligo, Ireland, 213, 270, 271
Somerset, England, 42
South Africa, 136, 266

South America, 57–58, 59–60, 61–62, 117–18, 120, 121, 156, 158, 159, 160–62, 163–64, 175, 176–77, 178, 179–80, 219, 220, 225, 250, 251–52
Soviet Union, 106–07, 116, 124, 146, 147, 148, 149
Soweto, South Africa, 136
Spain, 122, 153, 190-91, 276
St. David's Cathedral, Wales, 246
St. John's, Newfoundland, Canada, 200
St. Michael's Church, Vienna, 240
Stonehenge, 40, 41, 43, 269
Sucre, Bolivia, 225
Sulawesi, Indonesia, 247
Tahiti, 205
Tanzania, 111
Taormina, Sicily, 115
Tasmania, Australia, 144–45
Taygetos Mountains, Greece, 189
Temple of Apollo, Aghia Marina, Greece, 280–81
Tenderloin District, San Francisco, California, 190–91
Tenochtitlán, (Mexico City), 283
Thailand, 167
Thíra, Greece, 100
Thorung La Pass, Himalayas, 258
Tiananmen, China, 81
Tiryns, Greece, 64
Tokyo, Japan, 226
Tonle Sap River, Cambodia, 135
Trieste, Italy, 196
Tsabong, Botswana, 181
Tunisia, 28
Turkey, 68
Urubamba River, Peru, 59, 61
Uxmal, Yucatan, 53–54
Valley of the Camunians, Italy, 236
Varanasi (Banaras), India, 102, 217, 255–56

INDEX

Vecciatica, Italy 65
Venice, 169
Verona, Italy, 65
Vienna, 114, 240, 243
Vieques, Puerto Rico, 207
Vietnam, 108–109
Wailing Wall, Jerusalem, 82–83, 84, 217
Waitangi, New Zealand, 143
Wales, 57, 112–13, 245–46
Wat Arun Temple, Bangkok, Thailand, 167
Wat Than Temple, Phnom Penh, Cambodia, 134
West Java, Indonesia, 126–28
Western Wall, Jerusalem, 82–83, 84, 217
Wicklow, Ireland, 271
Wiltshire, England, 41, 44
Woodhenge, England, 41
Yalta, Ukraine, 148
Yucatan, 34, 52, 119, 248–49, 284, 285
Yugoslavia, 125, 151–52
Zanzibar, 194
Zimbabwe, 76–77

This book is the second volume of the Poems in Place poetry series and derives its inspiration from the poet's travel to exotic places. Both geographical place and the exotic within the poet's imagination are visited in the poems of more than one hundred contributors whose work is contained in this anthology.

The Poems in Place poetry series publishes poetry defined by either geographical or conceptual place. The third volume in the series, currently under preparation and edited by J. D. Smith, derives its subject matter as well as its inspiration from the creative talent and the musical genius of the Canadian pianist Glenn Gould.